VOLUNTEER BAMA DAWG

A TV Guy's
Love Letter to the South

To Patricia,
I hope you enjoy
this book!
Daniel Carroll
2024

VOLUNTEER BAMA DAWG

A TV Guy's
Love Letter to the South

David Carroll

Fresh Ink Group
Roanoke

VOLUNTEER BAMA DAWG:
A TV Guy's
Love Letter to the South

Copyright © 2016

Fresh Ink Group
An Imprint of:
The Fresh Ink Group, LLC
PO Box 525
Roanoke, TX 76262
Email: info@FreshInkGroup.com
www.FreshInkGroup.com

Edition 1.0 2016
Edition 2.0 2016
Edition 2.1 2016

Book design by Ann E. Stewart

Cover by Stephen Geez

Cover Photo by Mark Gilliland

Author Photo by John Collins

Photo Credits After Book Text

BISAC Subject Headings:
BIO026000 BIOGRAPHY & AUTOBIOGRAPHY / Personal Memoirs
LCO010000 LITERARY COLLECTIONS / Essays
BIO025000 BIOGRAPHY & AUTOBIOGRAPHY / Editors, Journalists, Publishers

Library of Congress Control Number: 2016954211

Hardcover ISBN-13: 978-1-936442-37-9
Soft-cover ISBN-13: 978-1-936442-36-2

Table of Contents

FOREWORD

Got Pudding?

A few years ago, I wrote my first book, "Chattanooga Radio and Television." More accurately, I put together a few hundred photos, then added some text and captions. Having no experience in getting a book published, I thought that once it came out, I would sit back and watch it fly off the shelves. I told my wife Cindy that since Chattanooga had so many notable broadcasters, the book had the potential to go national. She was skeptical.

Then one night, the phone rang. The caller ID display read "USA Today." I looked at Cindy knowingly as she answered the phone. "They want to speak to you," she said. I gave her that "I told you so" look as I intoned, "Yes, this is David Carroll. May I help you?" The caller asked, "Are you the David Carroll in Chattanooga, Tennessee?" "Why, yes I am," I replied as my head began to swell. "Great!" the caller said. "I'm Brad with USA Today, and we're starting home delivery in your neighborhood, and I can make you a great deal . . ."

So I didn't get any national publicity, but with the help of some book signings, it sold pretty well for a while. My life then took an enjoyable, if unexpected turn.

Some friends from a church invited me to speak at a luncheon. I asked if I could talk about my book, and bring a few copies in case anyone wanted to buy it. I put together a few pictures, some stories, and my usual warmed-over jokes. I had fun, and the folks seemed to enjoy it. One of the church members was in a local civic club which needed a program for their next meeting. This pattern continued, and I was soon involved in a multi-year banana pudding book tour.

You see, I spoke to more than a hundred church groups, clubs, and other organized groups. While I love speaking to all of them, I enjoy church groups the most. I know what you're thinking: it's because of the home-cooked pot-luck meals and desserts. Well, that might have played a small part.

Honestly, I don't know how I avoided gaining fifty pounds. Talk about all you can eat! Everything is made from scratch. At each stop, I was told, "We have the best cooks in the world." I couldn't argue.

But more than the food, I enjoyed making new friends. Each evening on the news, I talk about conflict, controversy and tragedy. It is refreshing to visit with folks who just want to share a few laughs.

At each of these events, they pray for their community, neighbors who are ailing or dealing with the loss of a family member, our nation and our world. Even when you're relaxing, you can't escape the fact that we live in scary times. Hearing their sincere prayers gives me a boost. They don't get much attention, but in every neighborhood there are hard-working people (even in retirement) who make our world better. They don't live their lives online. They stay busy helping their families, looking after their neighbors, visiting hospitals and nursing homes, and tending to their lawns and gardens.

After I tell my stories, comes the best part. They tell me about their lives and memories, and I leave knowing much more than when I came. They remember the first time they heard a radio, or the day their family got a TV. They tell me what their neighborhoods were like before the big stores moved in, before the traffic lights and four-lane highways. They tell me about the wars they fought, the children they raised, the grandchildren they adore.

I didn't expect to be do so many programs about my book, but I loved every minute of it. I am hopeful this new book will bring more joy into my life, and to yours.

CHAPTER 1

The Rock 'n Roll Kid

Glued to the tube at the tender age of two

You Can Blame Bob Barker and "Luther"

I wasn't born talking into a microphone, but I didn't miss by much. When I was growing up, friends and relatives would inform me that I was quite entertaining as a toddler. My older sisters Brenda and Elaine shared stories of how their baby brother would randomly greet a woman by blurting out the game show question of that era, "Would YOU like to be QUEEN for a DAY?" Even around the house, I would find anything that remotely resembled a microphone (a corn cob, a used-up paper towel tube), and go around interviewing people.

I was fascinated by our Zenith TV. There are several old pictures of me standing way too close to the screen. I was all too willing to be a human remote control, changing the channels constantly. After all, there were three to choose from!

My sisters taught me to read long before I started school, so it's probably no surprise that my favorite thing to read was the weekly TV Guide magazine. For many, many years, my weekly allowance was 16 cents, which happened to the price (including tax) of TV Guide. I never said I was normal.

My parents, Hoyt and Ruth Carroll opened a general store in Bryant, Alabama when I was six, and I finally found the audience I had craved. My favorite programs were the game shows, and I had begun impersonating hosts like Bob Barker as soon as I could speak.

At the same time, I carefully studied the hard working people who entered our store. Many of them worked on construction projects, or operated chainsaws in lumber yards. More than a few of them were missing a finger or two.

Bob Barker, game show host and career role model

Then I would see Bob Barker on that game show stage. Think about it: his job consisted of giving away prizes, and getting hugged by women. He wore clean white shirts, expensive suits, and he never had a hair out of place. Plus, he had all of his fingers. I counted them, just to be sure.

As soon as I was able to add up a grocery order, in full game-show mode, I would call out to everyone within earshot, "This roll of toilet paper is only FORTY-NINE cents!" At checkout time, I would announce to an unsuspecting customer, "Your grand total is, FOUR dollars, and TWENTY-SEVEN cents. Congratulations!" My parents were not amused. "Son, this is not a game show!" Well, it was close enough for me. Besides, the price was always right.

My specialty, however was stocking the shelves. I loved opening a box of Campbell's Soup, stacking each can on the shelf, with labels facing front, and dusting those shiny silver tops. I may have enjoyed it too much. One day as I dutifully performed this chore, my father said, "David, we need you up front. Mrs. Smith has several bags to carry out." I reluctantly left my post to help her out. I then resumed my can-stacking activity, but moments later my mother said, "David, there are some cars lined up at the gas pump, we need you out there." I rolled my eyes, and dealt with yet another interruption. I returned to the soup cans, and you guessed it, Dad said, "Son, we need you to carry some bags of feed for Mr. Morgan." I'd reached my limit. My ten-year-old brain exploded, and I said, "Dad, if these customers would stop coming in, I could get some work done!" After a few seconds of silence, my father pulled me aside and explained why it's never a good idea to complain about customers entering our store. As I recall, he said when they stop coming in, I would not get any money, ever again. That was my first, and most effective lesson about the world of retail.

I guess it's no wonder I adopted broadcasting as a profession. As a pre-teen, I would call radio disc jockeys, and ask them about their glamorous profession. Even as they complained about their long hours and low salaries, I only heard this: they were getting paid to play records and talk to girls on the phone. After watching my dad do oil changes and lift heavy bags of feed, I could hear radio calling my name.

I had heard about a guy named Luther. Before I knew he was a Chattanooga broadcasting legend, I knew that this Luther fellow had the power to close schools when it snowed. Of course, he really didn't, but it seemed that way. People would come into our store and stock up on bread and milk, saying "Luther said snow is coming!" The only Luther I knew was our Colonial Bread delivery man, and I couldn't figure out why he was such an expert on weather.

Luther Masingill, Chattanooga radio legend pictured in the 1960s

Eventually I learned that Luther Masingill was on WDEF radio each morning, and he was the Luther everybody was listening to. He was the most famous person on radio, so I called him at home one Sunday night. Here I was, a 12-year-old Alabama kid, asking advice from a total stranger. Even though I was interrupting his family time, he kindly advised me to read the newspaper, study English and history, and keep up with politics. At the end of our chat, he asked, "By the way son, where did you say you were from?" "Bryant, Alabama," I drawled. "I see," he replied. "Well, you may want to work on that accent too."

As soon as I was old enough to get some wheels (a Suzuki 100 motorcycle), I began bugging the managers of the nearest radio station, WEPG in South Pittsburg, Tennessee. I would hang out in the control room, hoping that one day the disc jockey on duty would get a stomach ache, and say, "Here, kid. You'll have to take over."

That never happened, but eventually the Sunday afternoon guy quit rather suddenly, and they were desperately seeking a replacement. I think they figured, "Hey, if we pay the Carroll kid to come in on Sundays, maybe he'll stop bothering us the rest of the week."

I'll never forget that fateful phone call. "Would you be interested in working Sunday afternoons for a dollar-sixty an hour?" In my mind I was thinking, "Heck, I can pay you more than that!" Just like that, I was a broadcaster. Even better, a rock 'n roll disc jockey.

Tales of a Teenage Disc Jockey

At the microphone at WEPG in South Pittsburg, Tennessee

Having started as a broadcaster at 16, my career has now spanned a few generations. It doesn't seem that long ago, when people would come up to me and say, "I grew up listening to you on the radio." A few years passed, and I would hear, "My parents used to listen to you on the radio." Now it's getting scary. "Excuse me sir, but my ancestors heard you on something called a radio."

Yes, it's been a long time ago, but the memories are still fresh. I can't tell you how many times people have said, "Why don't you share some stories of your early days as a teenage disc jockey? I can't tell you, because it hasn't happened. But if it had, I'd start with this one.

I had done the Sunday afternoon show at WEPG for about four weeks. The show that preceded mine was in an adjoining studio, where church groups performed. Through the glass, I could see the preacher, the pianist, and the singer, but I wasn't really paying attention. I was picking out songs by the Stones, the Who, and Lynyrd Skynyrd to start my show. If I got to the station a few minutes early, I would use that time to gulp down the bologna sandwich and Moon Pie my mom had packed for my six-hour show. At the same time, I was reading the sports page.

As the church group was winding down, the preacher began his goodbyes. "Brothers and sisters, before we leave the airwaves, I just want to say something about that young brother in the next studio. Brother David Carroll is just sixteen years old, but he helps us with the microphones, and then helps us carry out our equipment. I'd like to honor this young brother, by letting him deliver our closing prayer."

I almost choked on my sandwich. "You want me to do WHAT?" I didn't say it out loud, but I'm sure my fear-stricken face reflected that emotion. After about five seconds of silence, (it seemed like a minute), he repeated his request. "Go ahead young man, give thanks to the Lord." Let me be clear: I had never prayed publicly. Still, *I was on live radio.* There is nothing worse than dead air. So, summoning all my courage, and my best recollection of what people said in church, I mumbled something about "Father, we thank you for this food . . . um, that sure was a good service, and we thank you for that, and uh, well, be safe and have a good day and Amen." Now I don't know if that's exactly what I said, but I'm sure it wasn't any better than that.

It was certainly not my best moment as a broadcaster, but it taught me a lesson: be ready for *anything.* Ever since that day, I've tried to make sure that I'm never caught by surprise, when I'm on live TV or radio. It didn't seem like it at the time, but my prayer "blooper" was a blessing in disguise. So I'm giving thanks for that, here and now.

By the ripe age of 19, I was doing the afternoon show at WFLI in Chattanooga. During my days in South Pittsburg, I had perfected the art of doing hourly transmitter meter readings far in advance. According to that important-looking paper on the clipboard, the Federal Communications Commission required this meticulous monitoring. But, since the FCC inspector had not yet paid me a visit, I didn't worry about it. I would take a quick glance at the meters early in my four-hour shift, and write down the numbers in advance so I wouldn't be bothered with it again. I could then get back to the serious business of playing Bee Gees songs, and talking to girls on the phone.

Besides, I didn't know what those numbers meant anyway. Back then, a deejay could pursue either of two FCC radio licenses. A first-class license was for smart guys, the engineers. They usually had to go to school and take special courses in order to pass the test. My choice, the third-class license only required memorization of facts and figures that were easily learned, and quickly forgotten. Passing that test enabled teenagers who had never changed a light bulb to suddenly take control of a radio station. I was at best, a third-class radio guy.

Custom-built, water-cooled WFLI Chattanooga 50,000-watt transmitter,
feared by young disc jockeys

I didn't like to spend a lot of time near the WFLI transmitter. It was a huge, scary contraption with ominous red buttons, giant switches that looked like they could shut power off to the entire city, and "Caution!" signs everywhere. Each day I had to raise the power from 1,000 watts to 50,000 watts. I had no real-life preparation for this task. I merely followed the step-by-step directions, and hoped for the best. I would know I had raised the power correctly when the folks who lived the near the station would call to complain that they were hearing us on their toaster, their bedsprings, and their tooth fillings.

One afternoon, I started my shift at 2:00, took that ten-second stroll to the transmitter, and wrote down the meter readings for 3:00, 4:00, 5:00 and 6:00. As usual, I varied the numbers a wee bit, so that it looked like the 4:00 numbers were slightly different from the 3:00 readings, and so on. That way, if anyone ever really looked at the chart the next day, they would think I had been doing my job.

At about 2:55, the station owner, Billy Benns paid a rare visit to the control room, accompanied by his companion, a large

German Shepherd named King. It was a Friday, and Mr. Benns, who was known to be somewhat cranky, was especially irritated on Fridays when he had to sign the paychecks. Mr. Benns, who had assembled that transmitter piece by piece, was an engineering genius. Among the deejays, Mr. Benns was respected, and feared. Mostly feared.

He put on his glasses, found the clipboard and looked at the transmitter log, studying it intensely. I tried to stay cool, tapping my feet and swaying to the beat of "Rock the Boat." But I knew I was busted. He put down the clipboard and said, "Uh . . . Mr. Carroll." (He addressed all of us kid deejays formally, which I found very flattering.) "Do you have a crystal ball? Can you predict the future?"

Using my well-honed ad-libbing skills, I mumbled, "Uh, sir, well I uh, you know, it's funny you should ask . . . "Before I could continue sputtering, he asked, "How do you know what the meter readings will be at 4:00? At 5:00? That's several hours from now, Mr. Carroll." I'm sure I had a really clever comeback ready to go, but he continued.

"You know the FCC could shut us down for this, right Mr. Carroll? And you would be out of a job. I don't think you should let this happen again." I was about to pledge my newly found devotion to hourly meter readings when he grabbed the door, turned around and said, "And you need to start playing more Elvis. Let's go, King."

"Yes sir, Mr. Benns." He walked out, and I cued up "Burning Love."

There was also the time I met some cheerleaders at a fast food place. I was doing a remote broadcast, giving away albums and t-shirts, when they invited me to their pep rally the following Friday morning. "It would mean so much to us if you got up on stage, got everybody fired up, and gave away some albums," they said.

I gladly accepted the invitation. After all, that was the fun part of the job, visiting schools, and giving away prizes.

That Friday morning, I loaded up a box with albums by Journey, Styx, and all those other 80s super groups, and headed for the high school. The cheerleaders greeted me at the door and escorted me to the gym, where I marched on stage, carrying all those albums. As the students were being seated, a lady tapped me on the shoulder. "The principal would like to see you," she said.

The pep rally was still a few minutes away, so I jauntily headed to the principal's office. I figured he was going to thank me for taking time out of my schedule to visit his school, spreading joy and love.

I was greeted by the menacing glare of an older, obviously angry man. "What do you think you're doing here?" he demanded. I stuttered, "Excuse me?" It looked like smoke was coming out of his ears, and the veins on his neck were about to pop. "Do you think you can just come in here and take over my school?" he shouted. I said, "Well, I just came to give away some, uh, you know the cheerleaders invited me to . . ."

"Well nobody told me about it!" he yelled. "You need to get out of here now!" Always good at taking a subtle hint, I turned tail and left the building. I didn't even go back to the gym to get those albums. I figured someone would give them away.

A few days later, I ran into those cheerleaders again. "What happened to you?" they asked. "We looked around, and you were gone!" I guess they never got the word.

Now, all these years later, in my current job as an education reporter, I still visit that school quite often. The old principal's portrait still hangs on the wall, near the front entrance. I stop, smile and wave at his picture every time, to commemorate the first (but not the last) time I got thrown out of a school.

TV: It All Started with a McDonald's Commercial

My long career in the TV business was never a part of my plans. If you had asked the teenage me, "What will you be doing four decades from now?" I would have said, "Running a business and doing some radio on the side."

Of course, it didn't work out that way. The more time I spent at the microphone, the more I loved it. After a few years on AM radio, I was honored to be the first morning deejay on a new 100,000 watt FM station, KZ-106 in Chattanooga. That's where I met my future wife Cindy, then a radio newscaster. Certainly I had made the right career choice. My radio pals and I would go to lunch in our t-shirts and jeans, and see the other men wearing ties. "Man we're lucky," we would say. "We don't have to wear ties!"

My life took an unexpected turn in the spring of 1983. Someone from WTVC Channel 9 called and asked if I'd be interested in doing a series of car giveaway commercials for McDonald's, to be taped on six consecutive Saturdays. They didn't allow their newscasters to do commercials, and their only salesperson with on-air experience, Jerry Lingerfelt was already obligated to a car dealer ("we're open around the clock, until Saturday midnight!" he would exclaim, waving his arms clockwise). So they reached out to a shaggy-haired, bearded morning DJ. They set me up with a snazzy red McDonald's jacket and paid me a much-appreciated fifty bucks a week. Six Saturdays went by, the commercials ran, and I had a new jacket, $300, and six minutes of television experience under my belt.

A few weeks later, I got another call, this time from WDEF Channel 12. The program director, Doris Ellis asked me to go to lunch. I was greeted by Doris and the station manager, Gary Bolton. What could this be about?

"We'd like you to co-host the Morning Show," Doris said. "We saw you on those McDonald's commercials, and we think you could do a good job." "Sure," I said, "I'll try anything once. What day would you like me to do it?" The program was a daily, 90-minute, unscripted live show, and I figured I they wanted me to fill in for a day.

"No, you don't understand," Doris said. "We'd like you to host it, every day, from now on." The show had been founded by Harry Thornton, who had hosted it for 13 years before retiring a few months earlier. He was a controversial, veteran broadcaster, and the station found him tough to replace. The two guys after him lasted a combined nine months, and the Channel 12 people needed someone fast.

By this time Cindy and I were engaged to be married, and my job at KZ-106 was seemingly secure. What to do? Stay with the tried and true, or take a chance on TV? I'd always loved watching it, but never considered being on it. And yes, I'd have to wear a tie each day. In fact, I'd have to learn to tie one.

I did what any sane person would have done. I spent a quiet afternoon at my favorite spot, the waterfall trail at Cloudland Canyon State Park in Dade County, Georgia. Halfway down, there's a huge rock. There wasn't another soul in sight. I planted on that rock, and thought it over. I took my time, weighing the pros and cons. Ultimately I decided: I'm going to give this TV thing a try. If it doesn't work out, I thought, I could always go back to radio.

Me with Helen Hardin, Morning Show *hosts in 1987*

Truth be told, my sudden move to TV was an eye-opener. In a matter of weeks, this undercover disc jockey became a somewhat familiar face. My first taste of TV fame came at the drive-thru window. When I pulled around to get my food, a younger woman recognized me. She turned around and alerted a co-worker. "Martha, get over here! That's David Carroll, he's on the Channel 12 Morning Show!" Martha looked through the window, saw my face and said, "Yeah, I stopped watching it when he came on."

A few days later, my ego got a temporary boost in the super-market produce department. As I was squeezing tomatoes and sniffing peaches, an attractive young lady starting staring at me. At first, I dismissed her advances, but she kept getting closer. She finally worked up enough courage to speak. "Excuse me," she said, "but I just HAVE to ask you something!" My head started spinning. I've been recognized! I figured she wanted to ask me what it's like being a TV star, or about the famous people

I had met. "Sure," I replied. "You can ask me anything." With a sigh of relief, she said, "Thanks! Where do y'all keep your cantaloupes? I can't find them anywhere!" I realized I was wearing a white shirt and a red tie, just like all the store employees. She thought I was the produce boy.

Despite those brief setbacks, thirty-something years later, I'm still on TV. The Channel 12 gig lasted about four years, and then WRCB Channel 3 came calling. I made my last appearance on Channel 12 one day at noon, and went on the air at Channel 3 the same day at 5:30 p.m.

Sure, there are still awkward moments. Occasionally, I'll rush out after the evening news to make a speech somewhere, with no time to remove my makeup. As I tell the audience, "Look, I know what you're thinking. He's wearing makeup. Before you get the wrong idea, let me explain. I only wear makeup on TV. Or when I go to Walmart. Or church. Or when I go out and get the mail."

By the way, I'm still wearing a tie each day. Never mind how long it took me to learn to tie one.

My Granny's Gonna Love This!

Being a TV person, I confess to having a rather large ego. It comes with the territory. After all, if people don't recognize me, they're not watching, right? So it's always nice when someone makes a fuss.

Since I've been on TV for so long, it happens now and then. Some people call out my name, while others don't. They call me Darrell, or David Glenn, or my personal favorite, "You're that dude on the news!" Some people do a double-take. They'll glance over, see me, and their head jerks back as if to say, "Hey, I know him from somewhere." Others walk by, and when they think I'm out of earshot, they'll say to their companion, "Did you see David Carroll? He was the one with the mouthful of food, and ketchup on his chin." (They think I don't hear them, but we TV folks have enhanced hearing. That's how we get news.)

I saw a guy at the store. He looked me up and down, and said, "You look familiar. Don't I know you from somewhere?" I said, "I do the news on TV." "Oh," he replied. "That's right. I just can't think of your name." I said, "It's David Carroll." He paused for a second, and said, "No, that's not it. . ."

One day, I was sitting with a few of my buddies. We were blabbing away, when a young lady stopped at our table, and started zeroing in on me. As my head began to swell, she made it very clear that she knew me. "David Carroll!" she exclaimed, much to my delight. My friends were visibly impressed. By now my head was about the size of a float in the Macy's parade, and she squealed, "I can't believe I'm seeing you in person!"

I don't usually get the rock star treatment, so I was enjoying this. She said, "I've GOT to have my picture made with you!

Would you mind?" Modestly, I told her I would be honored to be in a picture with her, hoping my friends were taking all this in. If they didn't know it already, they were in the company of a Brad Pitt-like local celebrity, and they'd better be sufficiently impressed.

As she handed her phone to a friend, I stood up to squeeze in for a photo, which she would surely enlarge into a poster suitable for framing. We smiled for the camera, the friend snapped the picture, and she thanked me for this special moment. As my table-mates looked on, she shook my hand and said, "This is great! My Granny's gonna love this. Granny said she grew up listening to you!" As I sat back down, and my wise-cracking friends tried to suppress their laughter, I said the only sensible thing one could say in that situation. "Check please!" Oh well, I hope I put a smile on Granny's face.

CHAPTER 2

Friends, Family, and Favorite Places

Let's Go to Lake Winnie!

When my sons were little, these were the magic words: "We're going to Lake Winnie!" Somewhere in my unorganized box of VHS tapes, there's a video of Chris and Vince being rewarded for a day of good behavior by being told they were Lake Winnie-bound. What was their reaction? They would have danced on the ceiling if they could.

They must have taken after me. Throughout my elementary school days, a day in early May was reserved for the annual field trip to Lake Winnepesaukah, an amusement park in Rossville, Georgia. I didn't know it at the time, but that big Native American word means either "beautiful lake of the highlands" or "bountiful waters." To 3rd grade me, it meant the Arcade, the Tilt-a-Whirl, or the Mad Mouse, but it was a lot easier to say Lake Winnie.

I thought the Mad Mouse was quite a roller coaster when I was a kid. Until, of course the Cannonball made its debut. I rode it the year it opened. It sounded screaky and old back then! It still sounds that way, but that's part of its charm.

I've always snickered at the uppity folks who look down on Lake Winnie. "It's no Six Flags!" they'll scowl. "It ain't nothin' like Disney World," they'll sneer. "It's for folks who can't afford a real amusement park," some will say.

To those people I would reply, "That's right," and "Thank goodness!" Lake Winnie has never pretended to be anything it's not. As amusement parks go, it's on the small side. The sights, sounds, and yes, even the smells are unlike any I've experienced anywhere else.

During a ten-year period, I may have been Lake Winnie's most frequent visitor. As soon as my kids were old enough to experience the joy of sitting behind the wheel of a miniature car, we were there. I hadn't been to the park since I was their age. Oddly enough, I never took a girl on a date there, which was a huge oversight. I can prove that with only two words: Boat Chute. Where else can a young couple experience a tunnel of love, as the rickety boat makes its way up and around the track, in a quiet, joyous path of darkness, before descending into the lake, ending with a splash of uniquely scented water?

If you happened to be with a group of guys, what was more fun than sitting behind squeamish girls, lightly touching their necks while yelling "Snake! Spider!" That's entertainment, at a very affordable price.

Later, the park added a water slide, which became my new favorite attraction. The old Boat Chute usually resulted in a slight splash, but the newer water rides really do "Soak 'Ya."

As a parent, we had a plan: we would start with the slower-paced rides, like kiddie cars, then work our way up to the carousel and the Ferris wheel. We would then accelerate to the movers and shakers, like the Bavarian Bobsled and the Bumper Cars, where I'm pretty sure we loosened a few teeth. Our sweaty evening would end with quieter activities like the Sky Lift and Antique Cars, concluding with the train ride through the park. We all slept well on those nights.

For more than 90 years, this attraction has been the summer playground for the Chattanooga area. It's not uncommon to see busloads from out-of-town churches and schools, or a company picnic. The Jukebox Junction stage has hosted stars from both the Country Music and Rock and Roll Hall of Fame.

Adrienne Rhodes, granddaughter of park founder Carl Dixon, said the park has always operated on three principles: safety, courtesy, and cleanliness. She's right. The pathways are clean, and the park attendants greet you with a smile. Some of them have manned the ticket booths for decades.

Ms. Rhodes said her grandfather was a race car driver in the 1920s, and when he found the lake property, it belonged to a fishing club. He had a vision of building an amusement park, "and no one told him he couldn't do it," so he began with the Boat Chute before gradually adding more rides.

There's a place for Six Flags, Disney and the rest. Like many of you, I've been there and done that. But a part of me will always be at Lake Winnie. It put a smile on my face, my kids' faces, and it's comforting to know there are many more smiles to come.

Cloudland Canyon State Park: My Happy Place

Cloudland Canyon State Park, 2015

My love affair with Cloudland Canyon in Dade County, Georgia started in the late 1960s when both sides of my family started having reunions at the park. On summer Sunday afternoons, we would gather under a pavilion, enjoying covered dish treats while shooing away flies and bees. Someone would always set up a horseshoe game and a volleyball net. Of course the highlight would be a hike down to the waterfall. For us kids, it was an adventure as the older, braver ones would actually tiptoe around the rocks to get under the waterfall. For the grown-ups, especially those past a certain age, it was a badge of honor just to make it all the way down and back without requiring assistance.

I would always take along a radio. For some reason, those summer songs just sounded better with nature providing visual ambience. Even now, when I hear "Spill the Wine" by Eric Burdon, "Get Ready" by Rare Earth, and "In The Summertime" by Mungo Jerry, I'm back on the trails of Cloudland Canyon. It's wonderful how music from your youth takes you to your happy place, isn't it?

My wife Cindy is from Pennsylvania, so as she was getting adjusted to life in the South, I couldn't wait to show her my favorite places. Shortly after we married, we rented one of the cottages for an overnighter. No TV, no phone, just the sights and sounds of nature, everywhere. When our sons came along, we kept that tradition alive. Now it's their happy place too.

Each October I use a vacation day to enjoy what has become an annual ritual. I visit Cloudland Canyon to see the fall colors, and chat with people from all over the country who are there for the first time. When they ask me where I'm from, I tell them I grew up about 15 minutes away, and I tell them why the park means so much to me. I tell them that little has changed since I was a kid. Sure, we didn't pay five bucks for a parking pass way back then, but the improved facilities and maintenance are well worth that small price.

When we part company, those visitors always say the same thing: "You sure are lucky to live here." Yes, I am.

Blessed to Have Learned from the Best

Ed Carter teaching class in the 1970s

On the last day of school in the spring of 2014, Ed Carter called me with some big news: after 45 years at North Sand Mountain High School in Higdon, Alabama, he had just retired. The longest-running teacher in that school's history (a record I'm betting will never be broken) stepped down quietly, with no fanfare. Classy as always. He knew that year's graduation, the school's 50th, would be his last. "It was the seniors' night," he told me. "I didn't want to be a distraction." He wanted to do more volunteering and traveling, and spend more time with his wonderful wife Barbara. Why now? "No particular reason," he said. "I just think it's the right time."

That says a lot about Ed Carter. He's the very definition of the term "old school." It might have been hard for the class of

2014 to imagine a 66-year-old veteran as a rookie teacher, but it was easy for me. I was there.

In the fall of 1969, North Sand Mountain was in its fifth year as a high school, and was considered neighboring Pisgah High's inferior little brother. Those of us who lived in Bryant had a choice of high schools: we could ride a bus just five miles away to NSM. However, the Jackson County School Board also ran a bus 30 miles farther to Pisgah, due to popular demand. Many Bryant residents had graduated from Pisgah, and wanted their children to do so as well.

My sister Elaine had started her teaching career at NSM a year earlier, and encouraged me to enroll there in 8th grade, to get an early start at the high school I would attend (it was K-12). Compared to Bryant, it was a tough crowd. Some of the other 8th graders had been held back a year or two, and were a bit rowdy. On my first day, I got my first-ever paddling. An elderly science teacher liked to split up the students: he made girls sit on the left side of the room, and the boys on the right. One of the boys was making noises, and when no one would admit to it, the teacher just lined up the boys, and paddled us all. Welcome to NSM!

Meanwhile, a few classrooms down the hall, young Edward H. Carter was making his teaching debut at the age of 22. Fresh out of Jacksonville State University, he got off to a rough start. Most of the veteran teachers at NSM were laid back, encouraging a casual atmosphere. Discipline was spotty at best. Tardiness was not uncommon, and there were plenty of class clowns. So after a few hours of "Welcome Back Kotter" style behavior, we entered Room 16 and had to deal with Carter instead of Kotter.

His classroom was no nonsense, no excuses, and no fun. He was serious about teaching and learning. This did not go over well. Some of the older students began scheming to get rid of the rookie teacher. They figured if there were enough complaints about him, they could run him off. I'd seen it happen before in our rural community. A new teacher comes in, starts enforcing the rules, and before you know it, he'd be gone. So if you had told me in the fall of '69 that Mr. Carter would still be at NSM in the spring of '70, I would've bet against that. If you had told me he would be there for 45 years, I would question your sanity.

Most courageously, Mr. Carter took on some of the disgusting behaviors of that era. It was not uncommon to hear racial slurs thrown around in public, and in the classroom. Yes, it was inexcusable. You can say we didn't know any better, or our parents didn't know any better, and in some cases you would be right. But Mr. Carter wouldn't hear of it. He had zero tolerance for bigotry, profanity or bullying. He stood his ground. Sadly, few students stood up for him, because that was not a "cool" thing to do.

The heat would reach a boiling point each May. As graduation time neared, some of the slackers would express shock when they were informed they had not earned a diploma. They had failed Mr. Carter's class, having missed numerous assignments despite his frequent warnings. The young teacher wouldn't yield. The outcry was predictable: those students complained, and their parents complained even louder. But this teacher went by the rules. He had standards, and the students of NSM had better live up to them.

Against all odds, he outlasted his critics and helped change the school culture. During his 45 years at NSM, he taught thousands of students, including recent grads who are grandchildren of his first senior class. NSM is a far better place, and a nationally recognized school thanks to his influence. Other teachers had to step up their game to keep pace. After all, who wants to be known as "the easy teacher?" No one will ever say that about

Mr. Carter. He taught us the presidents (yes, I can still recite them in order, as can most other former Carter students). He taught us how to behave, and taught us how to succeed in college.

I've long given him much of the credit for my career. He was the teacher who got me excited about government, history and current events. Each day I work in journalism, I'm drawing upon those lessons learned in Mr. Carter's classroom in Higdon, Alabama.

He is the common bond among NSM graduates. Whenever I meet one, I always ask, "Did you have Mr. Carter?" "Oh, yes," they'll say. I'll respond, "Washington, Adams, Jefferson." They'll add, "Madison, Monroe, Adams." It's like our secret password. And with a knowing smile, we agree we were blessed to have learned from the best.

It's Election Season!

Growing up in Carroll's General Merchandise in Bryant, Alabama, we didn't see many celebrities. Occasionally, a Chattanooga radio star like Earl Freudenberg would stop in to ask directions to a gospel singing, but most of our traffic consisted of regular customers. So when someone wearing a suit and tie would come in, passing out cards, that was a big deal.

My parents were amused by my fascination with the local politicians. I was always disappointed if I missed a candidate who visited during school, when I wasn't there. One of the first politicians I met was Sheriff C.T. Dean, who would pass out "Junior Sheriff" badges to kids like me. I bet I still have mine somewhere, just in case I have to be like Gomer Pyle, and make a "citizen's arr-ay-est."

I would try to pry information out of the candidates, about themselves and their competitors. I remember asking one man why he was a better choice than his opponent. He said, "Why, that ol' boy can barely read and write, we don't want him spending the county's money!" (By the way, "that ol' boy" did win the election, and somehow Jackson County survived.)

In Bryant, we were proud of hosting the final political rally each election season. Our little community in the northeastern corner of the state reserved the Saturday night before the election, and we always filled the school gym. Even statewide candidates would make the long trip to Bryant, because the audience was far more than just politicians and their families. It was our big annual social event, and the Ruritan Club made extra cash selling snacks and drinks.

I enjoyed studying the different types of speeches. Some of the candidates were polished speakers, while others either had stage fright or just couldn't string together a few coherent sentences. More than once, I suspected a candidate had consumed a little alcohol prior to the event, trying to work up enough courage to face the big Bryant crowd.

One of my favorite memories is from a rally during which Sheriff Bob Collins was seeking re-election. Collins was the personification of the term "low-key." Unlike the cigar-chomping southern sheriffs seen in movies of that era, Collins was soft-spoken. At the rally, Collins' opponent was fired up as he took the stage, criticizing the sheriff, who sat behind him, solemn and expressionless. The challenger told the crowd he would clean up crime, weed out the bootleggers and increase neighborhood patrols. He ranted and raved until the bell rang, signaling the end of his allotted three minutes.

It was now Sheriff Collins' turn to speak. I remember thinking, "Man, how will he respond to all those attacks? I'll bet he's going to have a lot to say after the way that man talked about him!"

Instead, Sheriff Collins got up and said, "Folks, you know me, and I hope you'll go to the polls on Tuesday and re-elect me for another term." That was it. He sat down. I was amazed. He didn't even say his name! Of course, he won by a landslide, and won a few more terms after that. Who says you need a long speech?

This reminds me of an often-told political story. A congressman was at a political rally, giving his stump speech, which he finished to thunderous applause. He closed by saying, "Now go out and vote for me on Tuesday!" An elderly man jumped up from his seat, and yelled, "Not me! I wouldn't vote for you if you were St. Peter himself!" The congressman looked him right in the eye and replied, "No sir, you wouldn't. Because if I was St. Peter, you wouldn't be living in my district!"

Where Were YouTube "How-To" Videos When I Was a Kid?

I often joke with my sons about my tough childhood. The punch line usually involves how we didn't have a remote control for the TV set. "Yes, if I wanted to watch one of the other two channels, I had to GET UP from the sofa, and WALK to the television set to change channels." The joke, of course, is that compared to my parents, I had it very easy. They talked about riding horses on unpaved trails, and working in the fields dusk 'til dawn, and my sob story is about a remote control.

Since my dad came up the hard way, he learned how to fix just about anything. In the family store, I was usually assigned counter duty while he was repairing the freezer, the truck, or whatever had broken down. He was also busy repairing customers' chainsaws, changing the oil in their cars, or instructing them on which plumbing and electrical parts they needed. Then he would pass them off to me, where I expertly punched the buttons on the cash register, and handed out the correct change. To this day, I can calculate your change in a split second, but I'm not so handy with tools.

That is, until YouTube came along. There are "How-To" videos on just about any topic. Before YouTube, I had to learn to tie a necktie on my own. My dad showed me a couple of times, and with the help of a mirror, I figured it out after about 2,000 tries. Now you can go online and be an expert in minutes. In fact, you can learn ten different ways to tie a tie, which would be nine more than I ever learned.

The last time I bought a weed-eater, it was quite different from the one I'd had before. It came with a tiny, hard-to-read instruction manual. I took one look at it, and was more confused than ever. So rather than goof up right out of the box, I looked it up on YouTube, and a kind fellow had posted a video intended for a klutz like me. Suddenly I too, was an expert.

But my favorite YouTube how-to moment happened on a Sunday afternoon. Without getting into graphic detail, let's just say there was a toilet malfunction. It was the type of mishap my dad could have cleared up instantly. Me, I always called a plumber. But on this day, there were no plumbers available. I couldn't even find a plunger. Again, at the risk of giving you too much information, just know that this particular toilet really needed to work, and fast.

On my own, I couldn't think of a solution that wouldn't create a mess of historical proportions. My only shot was YouTube. I looked up "how to unclog a toilet," and sure enough, another nice man had posted a video. (Best I could tell, it was not the same gentleman who taught me how to use my weed-eater.) Thanks to some boiling water, and a little bit of dish soap, I was soon flushed with success.

Where was YouTube on all those occasions when I struggled to assemble baby beds, chairs, tables, desks, or anything that required instructions and a screwdriver? These tasks that most humans can complete in thirty minutes tied me up for hours. Most often, these projects only got done because I had put so many things on backwards, I would simply get lucky after repeatedly starting over. "There, that finally looks right!" my wife would say. "Now, leave it alone and go watch TV." I would gladly comply with her wishes.

Come to think of it, the TV set is the only object I've truly mastered. I've never needed a YouTube video to hook up cable, recorders, speakers, or to navigate those tricky inputs and channel guides. In fact, my father-in-law is convinced I'm a genius because I can always solve his TV problems. I've driven to his home many times, easing his frustrations in the middle of a cru-cial golf tournament. Keep in mind, this man has assembled many desks, chairs and tables, but is unable to master the mys-teries of his TV set.

I guess in a way, I'm his personal YouTube how-to video. Maybe I'm good for something after all.

A Salute to Uncle Owen

Owen Norris with his handmade replica of the White House

I come from a long line of carpenters and fixers. My dad, uncles and granddads knew how to repair and rebuild just about anything. Due to economic necessity, they did what they had to do, to keep the farm and household running.

That line ended with me. I need printed instructions to change a light bulb.

But if you need perfect cabinets, shelves or bookcases, my uncle Owen Norris is the master. Each year at Christmas, Owen builds something special for every niece, nephew, and cousin. He brings handmade, carefully crafted gifts, and never the same one twice. He brings bird houses and feeders, candle holders, and newly invented kitchen tools.

He builds amazing things, just because he can. One year, just for fun, he built a replica of the White House in perfect scale down to the tiniest detail. Another year he built a banjo, from material he found around the house.

When he sets out to do something, he finishes it. He is the first to credit his wife Kathie, who provides great assistance in his projects large and small.

Born in 1930 as the youngest of eight, he's among a special breed of Americans who grew up during the Great Depression. Most of us who came along later have experienced a few hardships and inconveniences, but Owen's family, like so many others, truly learned the value of a dollar.

Necessity was the mother of invention. Before Owen was a teen, he was helping his father patch up the family home in Bryant to keep snow from falling through the cracks in the crowded bedrooms. Owen's father (my grandfather Grover Norris) could build anything. Well into his 80s, he was repairing clocks. Owen still calls him the smartest man he ever met. Grover sure would be proud of Owen today.

By the 1950s, Owen left Sand Mountain to join the Army, where he served in Korea. When he returned home, he worked at Dupont in Chattanooga, as did many of his brothers and others from rural Alabama. For about fifteen years, he set aside a portion of his earnings into a savings account, with a goal of owning a business. His dream came true in 1969 when he and a partner purchased a lumber store, renaming it Sand Mountain Supply. As word spread of the store's hardware and Owen's custom-built cabinets, it became a huge success, and Owen stayed busy with it until he retired.

Our annual Norris holiday reunions, as captured on more than fifty years' worth of photos and home movies, haven't changed that much over the years. There are always plenty of food and games to keep everyone busy. I have video of Owen outshooting us all in a basketball game from decades ago. After having various hip and knee replacements, Owen can't outrun us anymore, but he still outworks us. With all those new parts, we call him the Six Million Dollar Man. Come to think of it, about half of Owen is younger than I am.

We used to line up the eight Norris siblings for a group photo each year. Now we have only Owen, who we appreciate even more with the passage of time.

He tells me he's writing a book about his early life growing up amid the dirt roads and horse trails of Sand Mountain. He has some great stories to tell, and I'll be the first in line to buy his book.

Uncle Owen, thanks for being a good son, brother, husband, father, uncle, grandfather and friend. You helped build and protect this country, and people like you have held it together. As long as you're around, we have someone who can patch it up when the cracks begin to show.

Daddy, What Did Greg Maddux Say?

At the age of nine, I discovered the Atlanta Braves. My uncle John Carroll took me to a Braves game during their first year in Atlanta. The Braves beat the Houston Astros that night 7-6, and I don't need Google to look it up. I remember every detail.

I've remained loyal to the Braves ever since. My wife Cindy would be the first to tell you, I've stayed with them through thick and thin, and in recent years it's been razor-thin.

Our sons Chris and Vince had no choice: they were tomahawk-chopping before they could walk. They were fortunate to grow up in the 1990s when the Braves were winning pennants, year after year. During most of that time, every fifth day Greg Maddux was on the mound.

Baseball Hall of Famer Greg Maddux

Maddux is the best pitcher I've ever seen. During his career, which stretched from the mid-80s to the late 2000's, no one compared to him. He spent most of those years with the Braves, after signing with them in December 1992. He'd just come off a 20-win year for the Chicago Cubs. Although the Braves had failed in previous years with some big-name free agents, I was cautiously optimistic that Maddux would be a keeper.

Boy, was he ever. He had pinpoint control. He worked fast, unlike some pitchers who were human rain delays. One Sunday we got to Atlanta a little late, and then circled the stadium a couple of times looking for a good parking space. Before we knew it, it was the fourth inning. By the time we grabbed some hot dogs and found our seats, it was the seventh. The game was soon over, in an hour and fifty-eight minutes. Didn't we just pay ten dollars to park a few minutes ago? Maddux didn't waste any time on the mound.

He could also field his position, with the cat-like reflexes of a shortstop, winning 18 Gold Glove awards. We now know he wasn't just a thrower, he was a thinker. He mapped out a game plan on each opposing batter, sometimes months in advance. He always had his own catcher, opting for guys who could read his mind. He liked Damon Berryhill, Charlie O'Brien, and Eddie Perez. They knew he was working on a higher level than mere mortal pitchers.

As Chris and Vince grew from toddlers to strapping young tee-ballers, they were mesmerized with Braves pitchers. They would study their pitching styles, and imitate their deliveries. With Maddux, I was afraid they'd imitate something else too.

On those rare occasions when he would make a mistake, he would express himself quite clearly. As baseball's TV audio got better, the field microphones picked up everything. Maddux would release the ball, the batter would make solid contact, and viewers could easily hear Maddux yell a full-throated obscenity. "What did he say, Daddy?" the kids would ask. "Luck!" I would quickly lie. "He's saying he had bad luck!" "Oh, okay," they'd respond, looking at each other like, "Well he is our dad, and he's never wrong."

A few minutes later, Maddux might make another mistake, and again the microphones would pick up his reaction, sometimes aided by a camera close-up. "#@&#@*%" would come through loud as thunder on TBS, as announcer Skip Caray would chuckle in response. "What did he say this time, Daddy?" Ever the quick thinker, I'd make something up. "He's really sad, boys, and he wishes his mother would bring him a sucker. Would you guys like one?" (Anything to change the subject). Soon of course, they would hear all kinds of interesting new words at school, and they realized I was a lying fraud. Thankfully they loved me anyway. Besides, while manager Bobby Cox was on his way to setting the record for being ejected by umpires, we learned several new vocabulary words, because Bobby made it easy for us lip readers.

It's important to note too, that Maddux pitched in the "Steroid Era," making his achievements even more impressive. He dominated hitters during a time in which many of them were chemically enhanced. Maddux's soft belly revealed a training regimen of cheeseburgers and Krispy Kremes. It's just another reason why this Hall of Famer is my kind of guy.

Will It Snow? If My Wife Tells Me So!

It was Sunday, January 9, 2011. Most people in the Tennessee Valley were either hunkered down with their weather radios, watching the TV weather forecasts, or standing in line at the supermarket. (When there's snow in the local forecast, and we see cars in Boston buried under five feet, our instincts tell us to hoard enough bread and soup to last until Memorial Day.)

For whatever reason, my joints and sinuses seem to be immune to atmospheric changes. Either that, or I'm just numb. However, my dear wife Cindy can detect a storm forming in the clouds over Chicago. I always turn to her when there are rumors of severe weather approaching. "Cindy," I said on that quiet Sunday. "How are you feeling? How's your personal weather radar?" "My head is killing me," she replied. I needed more information to decide whether to pack an overnight bag for work. "Where, exactly?" I asked. She pointed to her forehead. "It's above my right eye." I'd never heard that one before. "And it's really hurting," she added. "What do you think it means?" I asked. "Something big is coming," she said.

The next day, we awoke to ten inches of snow. The evening before, I had posted Cindy's prognostication on Facebook. It turns out she wasn't the only one. "My knees are hurting," one woman wrote. "My wife's right hip joint is acting up," said one man. Another woman wrote, "The vein on my husband's right temple is puffing up, and his headache is so bad, he's going to bed!" Others complained about their knees, ankles, shoulders and back. One of my friends wrote, "My left knee and ankle have been screaming snow since Friday afternoon!" While Cindy's built-in weather station was sending out alerts above her right eye, others felt the pressure over their left eye, and one man even felt it above both eyes.

"My husband says his knees haven't hurt so badly since he was a kid. My feet, ankles and the left wrist I broke in 2nd grade have been hurting all day," wrote one woman. "I've had a migraine for 24 hours," wrote another. And, "The metal plate in my neck hurts, so I'm stocking up on food now!" Others even talked about pain in their teeth, and changes in their hair. One woman wrote, "I know something is coming, I suddenly have a strong urge to clean the house." One of my male friends wrote, "I don't need a weather forecast. Whenever snow or ice is on the way, I get an uncontrollable urge to go to Waffle House. I think the waitresses send out some kind of secret signal."

If my human friends didn't feel the symptoms, their pets did. "I have a dog whose droopy little ears perk up when something is coming," wrote one man. Another wrote, "I have four nervous cats. They get like this every time." Some folks reported seeing blackbirds swarming, cows huddling, and squirrels stocking their pantries, so all the signs were there. There was even the distant sound of a train you don't hear any other time of the year.

So while the various forecasters and computer models have differing opinions on how much freezing precipitation we'll get and when it will arrive, Cindy just points to the big toe on her right foot. "I had surgery on that one," she said. "It's been stiffening up all afternoon. That only happens when there's a serious change on the way. Add that to the sinus pressure across my forehead and under my cheekbones. Something's coming."

I'm thankful for the Doppler, the Storm Track Radar, and all my TV weather friends. But when I'm too lazy to grab the remote, I just turn to my personal weather forecaster. I have now re-named her my Official Pinpoint Weather Wife 3000.

What's that, Weather Wife? Now it's in your knees? I'd better start packing.

Father's Day Memories: My Dad and His Wheels

There is a story about my Dad that I dearly love. I can't remember who first told me this story, but it was repeated at his memorial service in 2005.

Hoyt Carroll was born in 1922, the first of eight children for Floyd and Nell Carroll. By the 1930s, the family had moved from the rural Snow Hill area near Chattanooga, to the largely unpopulated Sand Mountain, Alabama community we now know as Bryant.

Like all poor families of that era, the Carrolls worked the fields. Oldest son Hoyt led the way, but on those rare occasions when an automobile would chug by on the dusty road, he would stop what he was doing to admire that car. "Someday I'm going to make enough money to get me a car," he'd say. I'm sure that seemed like an impossible dream at the time. But that was his goal, and he eventually got himself a car.

In fact, the running joke in our family, backed up by the truth, is that once he got a car, he couldn't stop trading. Back when the carmakers designed new models each year, he would trade up for the latest one. He was frugal and conservative in every other way, but he went through a lot of vehicles. Sedans, station wagons, pickup trucks, motorcycles, boats, tractors and motor homes. There was even a bicycle built for two. If it got from Point A to Point B with wheels and/or a motor, he wanted one.

Another year, another new set of wheels

When I was little, he shared his love of cars with me. Each September, when the new models were announced, we would plant ourselves in front of the TV. Chevrolet would always unveil their new models during the season premiere of "Bonanza." He was very proud that I could identify every make and model of that era, just by looking at pictures.

He might have been a little too anxious to get me behind the wheel. Inexplicably, he got me a motorcycle when I was 12. The reasoning behind that is fuzzy today, but my best guess is, some other boys near my age had one, and I probably begged for one too. For the first month, I was King of the Road. I was zooming up and down Highway 73, getting cockier by the day.

Unbeknownst to my dad, one evening I picked up one of my buddies and gave him a ride on my Suzuki 100. I learned that loose gravels and motorcycles do not mix. We had a minor accident, just enough to scratch up that shiny orange bike, and give both of us a few scrapes and bruises.

The pain from my injuries would be nothing compared to what Dad's reaction might be. Having a wreck, minor as it was, was bad enough. But I wasn't supposed to be hauling anyone around, at the age of 12. Let's just say he did the fatherly thing, and the Suzuki was grounded for a while. He often told me the loose gravels probably saved my life, because I was getting too confident, long before I had any right to be. As was so often the case, Father Knew Best.

A few years later, his love for cars came into play again, resulting in a choice I made that has been widely debated in my family. He got a good deal on a bright red 1965 Cadillac DeVille convertible, still the most beautiful car I have ever seen. By this time, I was a senior in high school. The car was about ten years old, but looked brand new. The previous owner put only thirty thousand miles on it. Dad thought this would be an ideal car for me, since I had been borrowing my Mom's car up to that point.

Believe it or not, I said, "No thanks." He couldn't believe it. "Son," he'd say. "When I was your age, I couldn't have dreamed of a car like this!" But much like that motorcycle from the past, I'd look at that shiny red convertible, and picture it getting banged up.

I also figured it wouldn't survive a school parking lot, next to other kids who were no better at parking than I was.

Later the convertible became his "parade car," which he often used during his time as a Jackson County Commissioner. I convinced him to get a less flashy car for me, which soon got banged up, just as I predicted.

He thoroughly enjoyed the give-and-take of trading cars, making every effort to squeeze the best deal out of a car salesman until one side or the other would give in.

I sure was lucky to have him in my life for so long, and yes, I hear his words coming out of my mouth when I advise my sons about cars and driving. Yet even though he was a strong influence on me, there's one area in which I did not inherit the Hoyt Carroll gene.

If he could see me today, with my 19-year-old car approaching the 223,000-mile mark, he'd say, "Son, don't you need a new car?"

Missing That Smile

My mom in the 1990s

Mother's Day should never be routine, but despite our best intentions, it happens.

If you're fortunate enough to live in the same zip code, you visit Mom. You go to church with her, take her out to eat, and buy her something that looks nice or smells good.

If you live out of town, you order a corsage, or you send flowers, and a card. Since my mom was always nearby, our Mother's Day included church, lunch, and a white corsage. Yes, it was a routine, but one that both of us enjoyed.

Now, several years after my mother died at the age of 90, I miss that routine. I see the commercials: "Don't forget Mom!"

"Be sure to call your Mother!" I feel like Bear Bryant did in those old Southern Bell TV commercials. He'd solemnly look into the camera and ask, "Have you called your Mama today? I sure wish I could."

I have friends who lost their mother at an early age, and I always felt sad for them when they would see those cheery Mother's Day commercials.

I have two stories about Virginia Ruth Norris Carroll, or as my dad called her, "Ruthie." One is kind of funny, the other one still makes me sad. Let's do the funny one first.

During my KZ-106 Chattanooga radio days in the late 1970s, I had just broken up with a girl, or maybe she had broken up with me. Either way, I was feeling down. Like many "newly sin-gle" guys, I started over. I grew a beard. Mom didn't like it. She missed my baby face, she said. For the next 14 years, she would frequently remind me how much she disliked my facial hair. "When are you going to shave that beard?" she would say. But I kept it, even into my TV news career. My wife and kids had never seen me without it.

One summer day, I looked in the mirror, got out the razor, and shaved my beard. I thought, "I'm gonna make Mom happy. When I go out to see her on Sunday, her son's baby face will be back, and she will be thrilled." You can probably guess what happened next. Mom took a close look at my clean-shaven face, scrunched her cute little nose and said, "You need to grow that beard back." Ah, mothers.

Now the sad one. I like to think I'm a decent enough guy, but every now and then, I fail at basic human behavior.

Mom was a child of the Depression, and grew up cherishing every bit of food in the kitchen. Those of us who came later had no idea. Food was in the stores, it was in our pantries, and it was plentiful. Mom was reluctant to toss anything out of the refrig-erator. One evening the smart-aleck jokester in me came out.

One by one, I would take a jar out of the refrigerator and make some wisecrack about the expiration date. "This one goes back to the Eisenhower administration." "There's something growing in this one." There were more knee-slapping insults. Anything for a laugh, right?

Then I noticed some tears on my mother's face. Her only son was making jokes at her expense. As soon as I realized what I had done, I felt very small. I had made my mother cry. I offered an awkward apology. "I was just trying to be funny, I didn't mean to hurt your feelings."

She got over my so-called comedy show. But I never quite recovered. It still resides in my memory like a fungus. She never knew it, but I spent the rest of her life trying to make that up to her. Long after Alzheimer's robbed her of her memory, I felt like I owed her so much. I could never do enough to make it right, but I gave it my best shot.

My sisters and I were fortunate during Mom's ten-year journey with Alzheimer's. She was cheerful and pleasant during her twilight years, just as she had been in her prime. My dad had been an excellent caretaker until he suddenly became ill in 2005, and died just weeks later. As a new chapter in our lives began, I looked forward to my weekend visits with her, taking her to church, going out to eat or just sitting at home watching the Braves. Later, my visits to her nursing home were just as pleasant. She always smiled when I entered her room. I know I will never see as sweet a smile again.

CHAPTER 3

Speaking Southern

Y'all Know Anybody Who Speaks Southern?

I haven't had my hearing checked lately, but maybe I should. After all, I was a disc jockey for about ten years, and I kept those headphones cranked up high. At our annual reunion of old disc jockeys, the voices keep getting louder, but the sounds keep getting fainter. I think most of us are reading lips by now. It's like that old joke about a couple of guys, both hard of hearing. One says to the other, "I just got a new hearing aid, and now I can hear everything! "Wow," says his friend, "Maybe I should get one. What kind is it?" The first man looks at his watch and replies, "Oh, about a quarter to six."

Of course, I've always had trouble understanding people. Maybe it started in our family store. Being raised in a rural Southern community taught me a language that was reinforced every day on TV. All those people on "The Andy Griffith Show" sounded perfectly normal to me. Later on, when broadcasting became my career goal, I realized I'd better work on sounding more like Johnny and Merv, and less like Barney and Gomer.

Greeting customers with Mom at the store in the 1960s

I remember some embarrassing moments from my country store days. I was about ten years old, minding the store when some folks from up north walked in. They looked around, and asked me, "Where's your pop?" I pointed to the kitchen in the back, and said, "He's back there with my mom." They looked at each other, then back at me, and said, "No, no. We mean, where's your soda?" I pointed toward the grocery shelves and said, "Arm and Hammer is on this aisle." They looked at me like I was crazy, and said, "No, not that. We mean soda pop. You know, like Coke!"

By then, I figured it out. "Oh! Co-Cola! Our Co-Cola box is over there by the window. We've got regular Co-Cola, grape Co-Cola, orange Co-Cola . . ." They hustled over, grabbed a couple of Co-Colas and went on their way, not lingering to chat much longer. I can't imagine why.

On another occasion, one of our regular customers, who I'll call JB, came in and said, "I need a batcher." "A batcher?" I replied. "Yep, where do you keep your batchers?"

I thought I knew where everything was, but he had me stumped. "What exactly is a batcher?" I asked him. He too, looked at me like I was crazy. "It helps you start your car," he said. My head was spinning. I thought he meant a key, or the ignition, which was all I knew about starting a car. "Hang on," I said. "I'll go ask Dad."

Dad was in the back somewhere, so I tracked him down, and with complete self-assurance, I asked, "Where do we keep the batchers?" He gave me that same look that was becoming so familiar. "The what?" he said. "Batchers," I replied. "Where are they?" He paused for a second, and said, "Son, what's a batcher?" I gave him that look that everybody was giving me. "It helps you start your car!" I said knowingly.

"Who wants one?" he asked. It was to the point of being ridiculous now. "What difference does it make?" I replied. "Do we have batchers or not?"

Again, he said, "Who wants it?" I said, "It's JB, but why does that matter?"

"Oh, now I get it," he said. "JB was in here yesterday and said his car wouldn't start. He wants a battery. I'll go get him one."

I was reminded of this recently when my lawn mower wouldn't start. I took the battery to an auto parts store, and it tested fine. But the guy at the counter had the solution. "It's probably your cellanoid," he said. "My what?" I said. "The cellanoid," he repeated. "They go bad sometimes. I'd go home and check that cellanoid if I were you," he said.

I didn't know what this "cellanoid" was, so I went home, Googled "cellanoid," and figured I'd get it replaced. I couldn't find it online anywhere. I guess all my cellanoids had worked until now.

After a little research, I found the word, "solenoid." It turns out, it's a switch that allows electricity to flow to the starter. And according to the dictionary voice guy who pronounces words on the Internet, it's pronounced "SO-la-noid," as in soul music. Except in certain auto parts stores.

Despite my hearing and comprehension problems, I'm glad some people still speak Southern. Besides, if my "pop" hadn't been in the store that day, JB would still be waiting on a batcher.

What in the Sam Hill Are You Doing?

I'm quite proud of my rural upbringing in Bryant, Alabama. My little community had only one school, one restaurant, and no traffic lights. We used to grow cotton, then flowers, and of course potatoes. I mean taters.

Growing up in my parents' store, I managed to avoid getting my hands dirty diggin' taters. I was busy pumping gas or running the cash register. That's where I met some real characters whose Southern-fried words are embedded in my memory.

Recently, I saw the musical "Million Dollar Quartet," which depicts the early days of Sun Records, with actors portraying Elvis Presley, Johnny Cash and Jerry Lee Lewis. At one point, a character shakes his head and says, "Lordy mercy!" My Pennsylvania-born wife Cindy looked at me and said, "Where did that come from?" I told her, "That's from MY neck of the woods."

Minnie Pearl, who spent some time on Sand Mountain in 1936, said she got a lot of her sayings from a local family. When I hear Minnie say "She looks like she's been rid hard and put up wet," I know where that came from.

(Speaking of Minnie, she referred to her brother as "Brother," like a lot of us did. Her best line: "When Brother tells you howdy, he's told you everything he knows!")

I used to hear people in the store say, "Can you put this in a poke so I can tote it home?" No wonder there are still stores in the South called "Tote-a-Poke." It makes sense to me, but I'll bet a lot of people under 30 have no idea.

We sold Ivory Liquid, but we called it "dish soap." Unlike the crowded dairy cases of today, we sold two kinds of milk: sweet milk and buttermilk. That seemed like a pretty clear choice at the time.

Many of the ladies would wait until 3:00 in the afternoon to come to the store. By then, the soap operas were over. Or as they called them, "my stories."

I knew some older gentlemen who never said, "thank you." Instead, they would say, "Much obliged," although it would sound more like "much-a-blodged" to me.

I was 12 before I knew that "directly" was the word I'd hear people say when they were telling someone they would arrive soon. It sounded to me like, "I'll be over there dreckly!"

I knew a few old-timers whose primary occupation was "piddlin." They would piddle in the morning, and piddle in the evening. They never seemed to get anything done, which I later learned is the very definition of piddlin. I have since become an excellent piddler myself.

Ask those piddlers how they were doing, and their reply was "hunky dory." That meant all was well. Especially since they weren't working hard, they were hardly workin'. In fact, some of them were "loaferin."

I never knew anyone named John Brown or Sam Hill, but I sure heard about them. Anyone who would express amazement would shout, "Well I'll be John Brown!" I never heard what the real John Brown thought about that. And if I ever meet Sam Hill, I would have to ask him why in the Sam Hill everybody used his name.

When they weren't talking about those guys, they'd say, "Well, I'll Swanee!" Somehow, I knew what they meant.

Cussing with real cuss words wasn't as popular as it is now, so I heard a lot of words that were the sanitized version. Shootfar! Dad-blame it! My foot! Well, I dee-clare! What in tarnation is going on?

At home, we never had "lunch." Lunch was served only at school. At home, that noontime meal was called dinner. When it got dark, it was time for supper. If you were lucky enough to eat out in a big city like Trenton or South Pittsburg, you were living high on the hog.

Nowadays, we think a lot. Back then we reckoned. "Reckon he'll be okay?" "Yeah, I reckon he will."

That guy who refused to do any work? He was "no count." In fact, he was "Pure-dee old lazy." I heard he was bad to drink.

If you got lost, you asked for directions. Your destination was usually "over yonder a ways, just past the holler."

Nobody from my parents' generation had ever dated, but they sure went courtin' a lot. If things went well, sparks would fly.

When a child didn't get her way, she would pitch a hissy fit, bless her heart.

If a little boy sneezed, his Mama would say, "Scat there!" That always helped shoo away the sneeze.

All these wonderful words and phrases, and the folks who uttered them, are "kindly" (kind of) fading away. Maybe you can help me keep them alive, by handing this down to your grand-young'uns.

Drunker than Cooter Brown

As soon as I wrote about Sam Hill, folks sent me more examples of "Appalachian English." I had listed a right smart of 'em. But some of you were "put out" with me, because I left out some of your favorites. So here's a big thanky for helping me recollect all the wonderful things "Mommer 'n 'em" used to say.

Many of my family's customers didn't come to our store to shop. Instead they "traded" with us. Although they were trading cash for groceries, that term dates back to when they would trade eggs, chickens, or corn. In return, they might get some "surp" for their pancakes, or some "warshing" powder. (By the way, you do know the White House is in Warshington, right?)

Before my wife Cindy moved down south, her only exposure to our way of talking was Tony Joe White's 1969 song "Polk Salad Annie."

She loved that song, but she asked a lot of questions about it. When Tony Joe sang, "She'd pick her a mess of poke salad, and carry it home in a tow sack," Cindy was stumped. "What's a mess?" That's a lot, I would tell her. Unless, of course, you were referring to a person who was a cut-up. As in, "That boy's a mess!" "Okay," she would reply. "Then what's a tow sack?" I'd respond, "That's a big ol' burlap bag." Of course, she would ask, "What's burlap?" I'd say, "Those are the bags full of arsh (Irish) taters." She would just stop and say, "I'll never learn Southern." Thirty-five years later, she's still trying.

To be fair, I don't understand half of what she says either. When our kids were wiggly, she would use the Pennsylvania Dutch term, "Stop rutching around!" And don't even get me started on "dippy eggs." Down here, they're sunny side up.

Speaking of food (which was kept in the ice box), about twice a year, we would enjoy "cracklin bread," sprinkled with pork. Another breakfast treat was a plate full of cat-head biscuits. Just don't eat too many of them, or you could get a bad case of what my 8th grade science teacher called "Dia-rear." That actually made sense to me at the time.

I also knew a peckerwood who would just lay out when he took a notion. (Translation: he was a lazy guy who would stay home from work if he felt like it.) His wife would say, "Get up off your hind end!" (Pronounced, "hine-end.") He'd say, "I'm fixin' to. But I'm just plum give out." (He was tired.)

In my previous story, I mentioned Sam Hill and John Brown, as in "What in the Sam Hill are you doing?" and "Well, I'll be John Brown!" But I forgot another famous name, reportedly the South's biggest party boy. When you heard somebody was "drunker than Cooter Brown," he was on a serious binge. Cooter was a real person, who lived along the Mason-Dixon Line during the Civil War. He had family on both sides, but he figured if he stayed drunk, neither side would enlist him. It worked, and Cooter Brown became a drinking man's hero.

There's more: when you were little, you might get a "bushel and a peck, and a hug around the neck" from your Momma. She'd finish it off by giving you some sugar. Not real sugar of course, but a kiss on the cheek.

If you were slow getting ready for school, your daddy would holler, "Shake a leg, son!" And if you were a little slow in general, he'd say, "Act like ya got good sense!"

These days, many of us get our movies from Red Box or Netflix. Back then, we went to the drive-in picture show.

Sometimes I'll close my eyes and remember a country store conversation, between a pair of good ol' boys. It went something like this:

"Boy howdy, look what the cat drug in! I ain't seen you in a coon's age! How ya doin?"

"Aw, fair to middlin. Some feller got sideways with me, but I beat the tar out of him. I think I whooped him, but he might've just been playin' possum."

"Well, son, keep it 'tween the ditches, a'ight?"

"Will do. Don't take any wooden nickels!"

"Don't do anything I wouldn't do. See ya in the funny papers!"

Look in the Chester Drawers

There is certainly no shortage of Southern-isms, based on the cards and letters I have received. Here's the latest batch. Maybe they'll tickle your innards. Let's commence.

We've already covered two famous folk heroes, Sam Hill and Cooter Brown, but somehow I forgot Chester Drawers. You know: "Where are my over-hauls?" The answer: "Look in them there Chester Drawers." "Oh, they were rat-cheer the whole time. I knew they had to be 'round here summers (somewhere)."

That story reminds me of an ol' boy. His bread ain't done. He's dumb as a box of rocks. Give him two nickels for a dime, and he'll think he's rich. He loves his ol' Shiv-uh-lay (Chevrolet). He orta get shed of that rattle-trap. One day, the po-leece pulled him over, si-reens blaring, and said, "Son, do you have any ID?" He said, "About what?"

I'm a little slow myself. Once I started following the Atlanta Braves, it took me a while to figure out why the guy squatting behind home plate is called a "catcher." Where I'm from, he's a "hind-catcher."

How many times did you hear this exchange when you visited the general store? "Howdy, can I hep ya?" "Yeah, where do yuns keep yer bakin' sodie?" "It's right past them cans of Vi-eener sausages."

In my family's store, we could always tell if a visitor was from above the Mason-Dixon Line. They would pronounce "salmon" without the "L," like "sammon." My wife assures me that is correct, no matter how many times I show her that "L," staring me in the face.

Ever since I was knee-high to a grasshopper, I was surrounded by candy in that store. It's a wonder I have any teeth at all. Or lungs for that matter. This was before the "no smoking" era, and we sold a lot of Luckies. Our regulars would stand around, smoke, and swap stories. "John, why ain't you workin?" "Oh, I can't work no more, 'cause of back trouble." "Do tell? That's turrible." "Yeah, the boss man said, if I ever came back, there'd be trouble." (Later, his wife would describe him as "triflin'.")

Here's another conversation I remember: "Speak of the devil! You still workin' at the fillin' station?" "No, I jest got farred." "Whut? You jest got harred last week!" "Yeah, but they farred me after I started a tar far." (Think about that one.)

There was one guy who was full of clever sayings. No matter what we were talking about, he would chime in, "Well, like the feller says, don't count yer chickens afore they hatch!" I always wondered who that "feller" was. Maybe it was Chester Drawers.

These days, kids act up on the school bus. That didn't happen when I was growing up. Mr. Dewey Cooper was my bus driver, and when some kid got out of line, he'd stare into the rear-view mirror, and say, "Boy, if you don't sit down, I'll bend you over my checkered apron." We never actually saw his checkered apron, but we lived in fear that one day we would. At least he didn't say the scariest phrase of all, which was often uttered by our parents: "Go cut me a switch," which was usually followed by, "Not that one. Go get a bigger one!"

Back then, if you learned something, you "knowed" it. If you got in trouble, your Daddy would look you in the eye and say, "Son, they ain't no call for that."

If you took off your stinky shirt after playin' down by the crick, your Mama would hand it back to you and say, "Son, smell of this! Have you been rollin' around with a dad-gum pole cat?"

The women's movement hadn't yet caught on, so it was not unusual to hear a man refer to his wife as "my old lady," even if she was 22! And if her husband preceded her in death, she would forever be referred to as a "widder woman." At least until another man "claimed" her.

Some country families used to have a lots of kids. One day, the census taker was making the rounds. At one house, a man answered the door, and the census taker asked, "How many children do you have?" The man started rattling off their names, and kept on going for a while. The census taker interrupted him. "I don't need names, just numbers." The man paused and said, "Aw, we don't use numbers. We ain't run out of names yet."

We'll get together again soon, good Lord willing, and the Creek don't rise.

Nekkid as a Jaybird

Buckle up, Buttercup. You may want to sit a spell, bein' as how folks have sent me some more Southern-isms. I figgered they would.

We used to get a lot of questions in our country store. Can I borry a tar arn? Got any chewin' terbacker? I'm getting' a mite hungry, where ya keep yer balonee? Oh, here 'tis, if'd been a snake, it'd a-bit me! (Keep in mind, we made a lot of "sam-witches" back then. There was no such thing as Mac-Donald's.)

We asked questions too. At the gas pump, it was "Which kind 'ya want? Ragler or high-test?" And if anyone made an ap-pointment, we'd always ask, "Are you on fast time or slow time?"

People would come in, looking for a plumbing part they couldn't quite name. "You got sump'n 'nother like this here doohickey?"

If a storm was approaching, you might hear your granny say, "Look out the winder! It's comin' up a cloud. I'm all tore up, it's scarin' the hound out of me!" We'd tell her, "Don't be a-feared of it, we need us a good frog choker, or maybe a toad strangler. We just don't want a herrikan."

You might hear a momma complaining about her lazy son: "I'm so flustrated. That boy ain't right. He don't have a lick of sense. I thought I learned him better than that. He don't care about diddly-squat. He'll just lollygag all day. I'll try to get him out of bed, and he's deader'n four o-clock. He won't hit a lick at a snake. He shouldn't act that-away. I ought'a just smack him upside the head with a wet possum. I told him, if he ever gets a whoopin' at school, he'll get another'n at home."

On the other hand, if there was a cute little girl nearby, someone would say, "They lawww! Sugarfoot, you shore are purty! Look at you in that yeller dress, sister! You're growin' like a weed. Goodness sakes alive, you're cute as a bug's ear!"

A Volkswagen was a doodle bug. You kept food cold in the Frigidair. It had a light bub inside that would go off when you shet the door. Smoke came out of the chimley. That part of your face between your eyes and your hairline was your fard (say it out loud). At the store, you put your groceries in a buggy (come to think of it, I still do). If you had put in a hard day's work, you were tard and tuckered out, but you still had to arn your clothes for the next day.

These days, "Sup?" means, "What's up?" Back then, it meant we wanted a little drink. As in, "Can I have a sup of your Nehi?" Today, we refer to a married woman as Mrs. Smith. Then, we called her "Miz-a-riz" Smith. Now, you get a haircut. When I was a kid, I got my ears lowered. People buy kerosene now, but in those days, it was coal oil. Today, if someone is nude in public, we charge them with indecent exposure. In those days, we would laugh it off. "He's nekkid as a jaybird!" Do tell?

Did you know a penny-pincher? "He's tighter than Dick's hat band." Someone you've never met? "I wouldn't know him from Adam." Or even better, "I wouldn't know him from Adam's house cat." Never mind that Dick might not own a hat, or Adam didn't have a cat. We know what you mean. We're not ignernt.

Speaking of animals and birds, we worked a lot of those into our favorite sayings. "That dog won't hunt." "I've got a crow to pick with you." "He's as cute as a speckled pup." "She's madder than a wet hen." "He's as stubborn as a mule." "He's grinnin' like a jackass eatin' briars." Well, this could go on 'til the cows come home.

If some guy was real upset, he'd get so riled up, he'd throw a conniption fit, especially if you egged him on. If a woman was in pain, she would go to the doctor to see if it was rheumatiz, or just her arthur-itis flarin' up. Sometimes it was just a crick in her neck.

Well, I'm purt near done, I've gotta skee-daddle. Be good, or the booger-man will get you!

CHAPTER 4

These Things Always Happen to Me

She Is Destined for Some Really Big Thighs

I mean well, I really do. But sometimes the autocorrect feature on my smartphone plays tricks on me. A friend sent me a message about her teenage daughter. "I'm so proud of her! She just won another major award." I intended to reply, "I've always believed she is destined for some really big things." But somehow, the word "things" became "thighs." Gee, that gives the sentence a whole new meaning. Sorry about that.

Same goes for this one: I meant to write, "I met this fine gentleman many moons ago." The word "moons" turned into "morons" and the result was not quite what I had in mind.

Overheard at the restaurant: A waitress said, "My doctor told me I have ADD-HD. I don't pay attention that often, but when I do, everything looks really sharp."

A senior citizens group invited me to speak at their next meeting. The lady asked me, "How long do you talk?" I jokingly replied, "Well, usually until people start falling asleep." "I've heard your speech," she said. "We'll put you down for five minutes."

Mick Jagger is now a great-grandfather. He is still doing stadium shows with The Rolling Stones, and is expecting his eighth child. My great-grandfather liked to whittle.

I have noticed that whenever a celebrity does something stupid, rude, or illegal, we know what will happen next: their public relations firm will write a sincere, heartfelt apology.

Overheard at the restaurant checkout. Man to cashier: "Why don't y'all turn down that $#@%#@$ music? It's too #@&%#@ loud!" Man's wife to cashier: "Ah, don't pay any attention to him. He needs to turn down his #$%@#$# hearing aid!"

Today's grammar tip: never end a sentence with some random, unnecessary word or whatnot.

It never fails. I'm in the checkout line at the store, and I run into an old friend. He's someone I'd like to impress. His cart is filled with fresh vegetables, fruits, and skim milk. Mine is loaded down with Cap'n Crunch, mouse traps, and a *National Enquirer*.

You know it's the wrong day to eat at the buffet restaurant when the first thing you hear is a mom yelling to her five-year-old, "Brandon! Get down off that salad bar!"

I sure miss the late Skip Caray on Atlanta Braves TV games. Back when the Braves were going through a long losing streak in the 1980s, during a rain delay, they would fill the time with a 3 Stooges comedy. Skip would say, "For the next few minutes, you'll see The Three Stooges . . . although you may not notice any difference."

I just read two interesting new health studies in the newspaper. One says eating too much junk food is bad for your memory. The other says . . . uh . . . where did I put that paper? It was here a minute ago . . .

My Own Steve Harvey Moments:
Favorite Mistakes

In late 2015 there was an awkward, embarrassing finish to the Miss Universe pageant.

Emcee Steve Harvey experienced what we TV people call a nightmare moment: he announced the wrong winner. It's why we sometimes look twice at our script when there's breaking news, just to be sure. The late Chattanooga newsman Roy Morris, when handed the bulletin about President Kennedy's assassination in 1963, asked his producer on live TV, "Is this for real?"

Harvey, a gifted host, had never made a mistake of this magnitude. In case you missed it, they had to take the crown and Miss Universe sash off poor Miss Colombia, on live TV! The actual winner, Miss Philippines, was understandably unsure when Harvey corrected himself. She wandered out in a daze as if to say, "Are you really, really sure about this?" It took a minute or so until she could force a smile, while watching another girl's dream come crashing down. To add insult to injury, that moment was seen later on YouTube by far more people than saw it live on TV.

Although Harvey caught a lot of grief on social media, his career recovered nicely. He was a good sport about it, even filming a parody commercial for the Super Bowl a few weeks later. Still, it drove home the point: these days, no mistake goes unnoticed. From the smallest town, to worldwide events like Miss Universe, if you screw up, the world will see it online a few seconds later. It's hard for me to pick on Steve Harvey, because my YouTube moment could happen at any time. The web is filled with TV newscasters doing or saying something stupid when they don't know the camera is on. I have made more than my share of mistakes while fully aware I was on live TV or radio.

When I first started in radio at age 16, someone at WEPG in South Pittsburg thought I could be trusted to read the local news. After I pronounced the word "indicted" wrong, they weren't so sure. How was I supposed to know the "c" was silent? I never made that mistake again. I was too busy making new ones.

That includes the time I emceed a big event at the University of Tennessee at Chattanooga, honoring the distinguished musician Dr. Monte Coulter. Many of the town's bigwigs were in attendance. I was trying to make my mark in Chattanooga, and wanted to impress the movers and shakers. It was my job to make the big announcement, introducing Dr. Coulter. I thought I was "big time" enough to ad lib it: I've never liked reading from a script. When it came time to say his name, I said, "Let's give a big welcome to the great Monte Irvin!" As everyone stared at me, I realized: Monte Irvin was a baseball player. I was supposed to say Monte Coulter. For some reason, the movers and shakers were not amused.

I even have my own beauty pageant blunder, although it wasn't televised. Still, I'll never live it down, because I still see the beautiful lady who was on stage at the time. I was emceeing the Miss Chattanooga pageant, and as each contestant paraded around in a swimsuit, I read about her hair color, hobbies, and so on.

Keep in mind that this is not the favorite part of the pageant for these girls: most are uncomfortable strutting around in a swimsuit, baring almost all. So the least I could do is make it easier for them, right?

A lovely young miss entered the stage, and I announced her name and her school. She got a round of applause and smiled. That's when I got mixed up, and told the audience she had green hair and brown eyes. Suddenly, the audience began to laugh. At first I couldn't figure out why, and then someone pointed out I said "green hair."

Now here's the kicker: the young lady was deaf. She had no idea what I had said. All she knew was, she was on stage in a swimsuit, and the audience was LAUGHING! Of course, most of them didn't know about her hearing impairment. She looked at me as if to say, "What is going on? Why are these people laughing at me?" Eventually someone explained it to her, we had a laugh about my mistake, and we've been great friends ever since.

So, believe me, I felt Steve Harvey's pain. Nobody's perfect, and when you make a mistake these days, there's nowhere to hide. Sure, he handed the title to the wrong girl, but at least he didn't say she had green hair.

Interrupting Jimmy Carter's Choo Choo Vacation

It was Friday, August 23, 1991. I was in the Channel 3 news-room waiting for something to happen. Suddenly, the phone rang. Was it a heavenly voice on the other end, granting my wish for a little nugget of news? No. It was just my old radio pal Bill "Dex" Poindexter.

At the time, he was managing the Gardens restaurant at the Chattanooga Choo Choo Hotel. Dex said, "Dave, you'll never guess who's eating a cheeseburger about twenty feet away from me." "You're right," I said. "Who is it?"

"It's President Jimmy Carter, with his wife Rosalynn, and their grandkids. They're having lunch, and then they're gonna get on the box cars," Dex said. He capped it off with, "And you're the only person I'm telling." I yelled to my photographer Glen Wagner, "Let's go, we've got a president at the Choo Choo!" Glen grabbed the camera, and we took off. As we got in the car, I told him about Dex's confidential tip. "Does President Carter know we're coming?" he asked. "I don't think so," I said. "I guess we'll surprise him."

Our nation's 39th president

When we got to the Choo Choo, there was nothing out of the ordinary. "Gee, I hope we didn't miss him," Glen said. There was no limo, and there were no Secret Service agents staring us down. A few scattered tourists were roaming the grounds. We headed to the restaurant area. We didn't want to barge in, so we took a quick look through the window. There they were! The Carters, ten years removed from the White House, enjoying a quiet lunch with the grandkids. "Glen!" I said. "Go ahead and turn on your camera, this may be all we get!" He dutifully aimed through the glass, and Mrs. Carter spotted us. I'm not a lip-reader, but she said something to her husband, like, "How nice! Those delightful local news reporters found out we're here on vacation! What a pleasant surprise!" Or maybe that's not exactly what she said. Anyway, Mr. Carter turned around, looked through the window, and looked me right in the eye.

He quickly turned back to his wife with that "busted" look on his face. Sensing his disappointment, I said, "I'll tell you what, Glen. Let's give them time to eat, and do some sightseeing, and then I'll ask him for an interview." It turns out there were a couple of Secret Service guys who politely requested we give the President "a little space." Fearing a headline of "Alleged news guy ruins presidential vacation," I gladly consented.

Glen and I waited, and our persistence was rewarded. About a half-hour after finishing their meal, the Carter family had wrapped up their tour of the complex. The grandchildren had hopped on and off every box car in sight, so I said to Glen, "Here's our chance!" I walked up to Mr. Carter, shook his hand, and introduced myself.

"Mr. President," I said, "I really hate to bother folks when they're on vacation . . ." He stopped me in mid-sentence, flashed that famous grin, and said, "It must not bother you too much." I laughed awkwardly. (Was he kidding? Or did I just play Fail to the Chief?) I plodded on. "If you can spare a minute for a quick interview . . ." He stopped me again. "As long as it's quick, because we're ready to go home." I can take a hint. Fortunately, Glen worked fast, and we were ready to roll.

After that rough start, he couldn't have been any nicer. I had my questions ready. Could there be a female presidential candidate in 1992? Absolutely, he said. There were several qualified women. Did he expect a big-name politician to win the '92 Democratic nomination (Al Gore, Jerry Brown and Mario Cuomo were front-runners at the time), or would it be a relative unknown, as he had been in 1976? He said the election was still 15 months away, and there was plenty of time for a lesser-known candidate to emerge, (It ended up being an obscure southern governor named Bill Clinton. Whatever happened to him?)

He also commented on his knowledge of downtown Chattanooga, the railroads, and even the quality of his lunch. He didn't seem too annoyed as we parted company, and I had my exclusive interview for the 6:00 news.

Mr. Carter returned to the area in 2014, to campaign for his grandson Jason, who was running for governor of Georgia. When I heard he was coming, I called Dex. "I just wanted to thank you again for tipping me off that day Jimmy Carter came to the Choo Choo," I said. "Yeah, I'll never forget that day," Dex said. "I told the staff to take good care of him and his family, and after a while, I went to the bathroom. There was somebody in the next stall, and I realized it was him. That was the first time I met a sitting president."

It's My Kenny Rogers Story, and I'm Sticking to It.

The Gambler himself, Kenny Rogers

Recently I heard a Kenny Rogers song on the radio, and then I read a wonderful story about him. "The Time of My Life" is a book by Bill Medley, the deep-voiced half of the Righteous Brothers (with tenor Bobby Hatfield). Back in 1964, they recorded the most-played song in the history of radio. "You've Lost That Lovin Feeling" sounds like no other song. Deejays wouldn't play it when it came out, because when Bill sang those opening words, "You never close your eyes any more, when I kiss your lips . . ." they thought it was recorded on the wrong speed!

Eventually they figured it out, listeners loved it, and it sold millions. The Righteous Brothers became one of the hottest acts in the nation. They befriended a newcomer named Kenny Rogers, and helped him in the early days of his career.

A few years later, it was Kenny having all the hits, while the Righteous duo faded from the charts. In Bill's book, he writes about falling on lean financial times, after making some poor investments. By this time, Kenny was pumping out gold records like "Lucille," "Coward of the County," and "The Gambler." Bill asked Kenny for a $20,000 loan. "I promise to pay you back as soon as I can," he said. Kenny pulled out his checkbook, and wrote him a check for $20,000. "This is not a loan, it's a gift," he said. Bill protested, but Kenny said in a non-boastful way, "Do you know how much money I'm making? You would do the same thing for me." A few weeks later, Bill tried to pay him back. Kenny handed back the envelope. Bill said, "I'm paying you back, you loaned me 20 grand." Kenny emphasized that it was not a loan, and refused to take the money back. What a guy.

That reminded me of another first-hand report of Kenny's kindness. In the WFLI "Jet-FLI Spectacular" days of all-star 1960s concerts at Chattanooga's Memorial Auditorium, station manager Johnny Eagle recalled how difficult it was to get someone to open the show. They all wanted to be the headline act, and close the show. Johnny said, "Kenny Rogers made it easy for me. He was among the nicest stars. He even carried his own equipment. I'd go up to Kenny, kind of embarrassed, and ask him if he would be kind enough to open the show, and he'd say absolutely, whatever you need. He had more hits than anybody, but he didn't act like it. It was no surprise to me that he went on to be more successful than any of them."

In the early 1980s, when I was music director for KZ-106, Kenny released a new album on Liberty Records. Record promoter Bob Alou visited the station, and asked us to play

Kenny's songs. Bob was well known in the industry as a bit of a wild man. Still, one afternoon, I accepted his invitation to take a ride through Chattanooga, just long enough to hear Kenny's new album (on cassette) on his car stereo. As he drove through the downtown streets, he decided to light up a joint. He would take long, deep drags, and he was determined to finish the joint before we returned to the radio station. He'd crank up Kenny's songs even louder, saying "Wow that sounds good!" Thankfully, we were not stopped by the police. Even though I wasn't smoking, I was probably high by association, and my clothes smelled like pot. My wife Cindy understood. She had been in radio too.

In fact, that record promoter scored big points with Cindy just a few weeks later. Kenny booked a show at the UTC Arena, and Bob arranged for us to meet Kenny backstage. Cindy, by then a seasoned news reporter, started thinking about what she would ask him. "What will your next record be?" "Tell us about your new baby boy." "What do all those Grammy nominations mean to you?" She was prepared, as always.

After the show, we were escorted backstage, and there stood Kenny Rogers. Tall, tanned and handsome in his white suit. We exchanged pleasantries, and he thanked me for playing his songs. I nodded to Cindy, as if to say, "Your turn." She was so taken aback by his good looks, she could not speak. A few words came out, but not in the right order. She was star struck. Kenny smiled and said, "Well, it sure was nice to meet you." Cindy turned three shades of red, and said, "Kerfuffle perdunkin," or something like that. I'd never seen her speechless, before or since. ("I didn't expect him to be so handsome!" she would say later.)

Kenny Rogers then walked away, sporting a big smile. It surely wasn't the first time he'd made a pretty girl blush.

We'll Have More Information When We Get It

When we TV news anchors look into the camera to bring you the news, we haven't memorized anything. We're reading it off the TelePrompTer, a nifty device that allows us to "look you in the eye," and read at the same time. This trick does not involve smoke, but it does utilize a mirror.

Over the years, I have developed a habit. I do not read the script from the prompter word for word. Even if I've written it myself, I usually change it, live on the air. I've convinced myself that I can make the copy better by ad-libbing, in an effort to make it more conversational. Sometimes, I succeed. But other times I say something so stupid that I regret it the moment it leaves my lips. I'm hoping no one catches it, but someone always does. One day the script read, "We'll have more information when it becomes available." I attempted to ad-lib, "We'll bring you more information when we get it." Instead, I blurted out this nugget of nonsense: "We'll have more information when we get it." Say that out loud. I hope they spell my name right on my Emmy Award.

I try to avoid cliché's, because they turn up on the news (local and network) an awful lot. My co-anchor Cindy Sexton and I grimace when we hear that "officials are tight-lipped." In fact, we tighten our own lips, to no avail.

If I had a nickel for every time I've ended a story by saying, "The investigation is continuing," I'd have some serious cash. I mean, that should be obvious. We all know that cops and firefighters aren't going to leave the scene and say, "You know what? I'm stumped by this one. Let's just forget about it, and maybe the whole thing will just blow over."

Sometimes we trivialize death. In the wake of a storm in Iowa, we'll say, "The damage to homes and businesses was extensive, but there was only one death." You know, to that person's family, "only one death" is kind of a big deal. The person started the day alive and well until that storm came, remember?

There are so many more. When we say, "Smith and Jones spent their day on the campaign trail," where is that trail, exactly? Are there markings on the trees? If we say, "canine dogs," should we also say, "human people?" Why do we say "a final farewell?" A farewell is already final, right?

I'm reluctant to say that someone "lost his battle with cancer." It is said with good intentions, but I've known many people who suffered from debilitating diseases. For most of them, the odds of a long-term recovery were slim. But once they passed away, I didn't feel they "lost" at anything. I thought they were winners for displaying courage and grace in their final weeks. They'll always be winners to me.

Have you ever heard about a structure that was "completely destroyed" by fire? Can something be partially destroyed? Maybe destroyed just a wee bit? Nope, it's either destroyed, or it isn't.

We've told you grim details about people who were "fatally killed" or "electrocuted to death." Some were in a "terrible accident," as opposed to a wonderful accident, I guess. We describe a "senseless crime" so you'll know it wasn't a meaningful crime. We tell you that an injured person was taken to a "local" hospital. Aren't you glad the paramedics didn't take the guy to a hospital two thousand miles away? How about "she's lucky to be alive?" After witnessing the miracle of birth a couple of times, and having driven in Atlanta rush hour traffic, I think we're all lucky to be alive.

Sometimes we use a lot of words when just two will do. Doesn't "totally engulfed in flames" mean the same thing as "on fire?"

The weather people, who ad-lib everything, let one slip occasionally too. From the Department of Redundancy Department, they'll say, "Currently right now in Nashville, it's 71." And instead of saying, "Old Man Winter is bringing on the white stuff," can't they just say that it's going to snow?

I try to avoid "literally" and "actually." I've heard reporters say, "Police are -literally- combing the neighborhood for clues." That must be one big comb. And if I tell you that "Mayor Johnson -actually- just presented his budget," isn't that one word too many?

Our own buzzwords have become cliché's. Remember when "Breaking News" meant something huge had just happened? For instance, a major earthquake, or perhaps an explosion. Now, the cable news channels, yapping for attention like puppies at feeding time, will trumpet their "Breaking News" banner to inform us that Justin Bieber peed in a mop bucket in the kitchen of a restaurant. I'm not making that up.

So that's the "very" latest. (Huh?) At the end of the day, here's the bottom line: it remains to be seen. Because only time will tell. But this much is for sure: I will have more information when I get it.

My Weird, Wired Life

You know what they say: "It always happens in threes." So it was, recently with three of my longtime companions. I lost my compact disc (CD) recorder, my home DVD recorder, and my work DVD recorder. Cause of death? A combination of outdated parts, and dirty, scratched heads. Sure, I could send them off to some mysterious repair service to be patched and cleaned, but at what cost? As every customer service rep is trained to say, occasionally in English, "It would be cheaper to buy a new one. And I just happen to have a deal for you!"

So, I removed the only parts with any value (the batteries from the remote controls), and thanked my old machines for their service. To be fair, they had high mileage. I started recording music on CDs before it became easier to do on a computer, and I'm still in the midst of a tedious project to convert my old VHS tapes to DVD.

I shopped online for replacement devices, found some good deals, and I'm thrilled with the results. My new machines work, for now anyway. That's the good news. You know what comes next.

While disconnecting and reconnecting all the wires and cables that go into the receivers, stereos and TV sets, I found myself with a few extras. Some came boxed with the new machines, and some of the older ones are no longer needed. As I was throwing the old wires and cables into my big box labeled, "Old Wires and Cables," I realized I now had more merchandise than Radio Shack. In fact, Radio Shack is only in business today because I have purchased the same cables over and over, since the early 1980s.

I'm a little tied up right now.

As I was digging around behind the TV, I found a huge plug, tying up two spaces on my already overcrowded outlet strip. After tracing its cord through a curled, twisted jungle of lookalikes, I learned it was attached to absolutely nothing. It was just plugged in, serving no purpose at all. I'm sure it had resided there since Ronald Reagan's first term. For many years, it had looked important, so I never touched it. I remembered all the times I needed an extra outlet or two. Of course, I will keep that mystery plug and cord, because I surely own something that needs it. Something valuable, like an 8-track player.

I've kept all those old wires and cables, because they have come in handy on occasion. My father-in-law lives down the street. He's still a proud VCR owner, and he thinks I'm a genius because I know where all those cables go. He will always consider me a genius as long as my repairs are limited to his video connections. If I'm ever called upon to fix his sink or his car, my reputation will be ruined.

My collection ranges from the wildly popular RCA AV cables (good) to the mysterious S-Video (better) to the 21st century HDMI (best). I have a bunch of those red, green and blue component cables too, although I've never used them. I've learned that the off-brand five-dollar cables deliver the same colorful picture that the big-name fifty-dollar ones do. I have all sorts of male to female extensions, male to male adapters, female to female couplers, and other scandalous combinations.

I have charging cables for cell phones like Zack used on "Saved by the Bell." I have those wide-mouth computer cables that Bill Gates phased out about 9 Windows ago. I have headphone jack adapters from an era in which a "pod" was where a pea resided. If any of these products ever make a comeback, I'm ready. In fact, if I connected all of my cords, cables and wire, and aimed them toward New York City, they would generate enough static electricity to make Donald Trump's hair stand on end.

Now that I've replaced my dilapidated old machines with smooth-humming new models, what will I do with all of these unnecessary connection cables? I think my first stop will be the returns counter at Radio Shack. I figure my collection should be worth about three stores.

Mail-in Rebate? Just Show Me the Money!

About fifteen years ago, I made a decision I soon came to regret. We needed a dishwasher. I could spend a lot of money, and get a quiet one, or I could spend far less money, and get one . . . well, not as quiet. Against my wife's wishes, I opted to go cheap. I mean, how much louder could it be?

Well, let me put it this way. If neighbors look toward the sky, wondering why a 747 is flying over Chattanooga . . . you might have a loud dishwasher.

For fifteen years, our TV viewing has been interrupted by the monster in the kitchen. It sits there grinding away, with water splashing, dishes crashing and loud slurping noises that sound like the Tasmanian Devil is snorting the supply from the Tennessee River.

It would hold back its loudest belches for the dramatic pauses on our favorite shows. "Doctor, did the results come back?" "Yes, and you'll want to listen carefully. We've never seen anything like this. We can say with 100 percent certainty that John is going to . . ." ROARRRR . . ." Yes, that's been life with our low-priced, thunderous dishwasher.

But like all cheap machines, it had an expiration date. That dishwasher has served up its last loud volcanic eruption. Unlike the loss of some household appliances, there were no tears shed in our home. Instead my wife laid down the law, as wives do so well. "This time," she said in tones that would have drowned out the old dishwasher, "we're getting a quiet one!" Just before ducking a potential flying frying pan, I said charmingly, "Yeah, like I wanted all along." I should have ducked a wee bit lower.

So on the next trip to the big-box store, my orders were clear: get the quietest one on the floor. Our friendly salesperson pointed to the most expensive one of course, assuring me it wouldn't rouse a mouse. But, lucky me! For a limited time only (maybe for the next ten years) I would get a $100 rebate!

I was handed a series of cash register receipts with graduate-school level instructions on how to apply for a mail-in rebate. Laid end-to-end, they would pave I-24 (not a bad idea). After following step-by-step rules on what to fill out, which receipts to send, and how to lick the stamp, I sent the bulging envelope to a small Texas town that probably has 37 post office boxes. Yet the intentionally confusing address looked like this: "Big Box Store Summer Dishwasher Beyonce Lava Lamp Gluten-Free Promotion, PO Box 4893659275692, Tiny Town, Texas 5745345-563463.

Now that I've paid full price for the dishwasher, they will do everything they can to discourage me from actually sending in the rebate form. There's a reason they didn't just knock $100 off at the checkout.

They're betting that I will look at all those receipts, the confusing instructions, and the complicated address, and then throw up my hands and say, "I'll do this later!" Or they're hoping I'll misplace the paperwork. Either way, they're betting I'll never get around to it. They've sold the dishwasher at full price, so they really don't want to hear from me, ever again.

Wouldn't it be a shame if I failed to remember one of those detailed instructions, or missed a number on that lengthy address? If I do anything wrong, they'll happily send a card with this message: "Your rebate submission was incomplete, or incorrect. We are unable to process your request."

Having been burned before, I took extra time and caution to do everything just right, and made copies of every page. Several weeks passed, with no way to track my rebate online, although their website said I could. So, I went back to the store, and a nice lady made a few phone calls and learned that yes, my rebate request had been received, "and was being processed."

Several more weeks passed, and my rebate check finally arrived. It's a good thing it did, because I was prepared to drive all the way to Tiny Town, Texas to claim my hundred bucks.

In the meantime, I did one thing right. I now have a quiet dishwasher. It may be running right now, I can't say for sure.

I Feel Good, I Knew That I Would

I recently walked out of my allergist's office, and said to my-self, "I feel good." Now, why waste your valuable time on my (*knock on wood*) good health? Because I've made four lifestyle changes that have made me feel better than I did years ago. Who knows, there may be someone reading this who wants to feel better, and perhaps I can help. I'm no doctor, but my first two initials are D.R. Close enough.

1) I finally went to the allergist. Ever since I was in my twen-ties, I sneezed a lot. I have vivid memories of spring soft-ball games, sneezing my brains out. My wife Cindy would suggest I see someone about it, but in typical male fash-ion, I'd blow it off (pun intended). I remember telling her, "It's no big deal, I sneeze every day of the year."

True, but it got to the point that I was miserable, and downright sick every May. The tree and grass pollen overwhelmed me. Then in October the leaves would fall, and my misery level would rise again. Twice a year, for several weeks at a time, I'd trudge on to work, on radio and TV, stuffed up and sore-throated. It was just part of life, I thought. Finally I had the "scratch test" done, the allergies were identified, and the weekly shots in the arm began. Soon they were bi-weekly, and eventually just once a month, before ending completely. It was easily the best doctor's visit I ever made. The relief was immediate, making this decision a real life-changer.

2) I finally went to the dermatologist. Being of fair skin and English/Irish descent, the sun is not my friend. No one told me this when I was a teen, sunbathing constantly in

a futile effort to look as good as my bronzed friends. No one said anything about it when I was playing softball under the sun, with no protection. I kept thinking that my painful beet-red burn would magically peel into a skin tone somewhere between Bob Barker and George Hamilton. No such luck. When I finally visited a dermatologist, he looked first into my family history, then deeply into my skin, and laid down the law. "Hey Knucklehead," he may well have said. "You shouldn't even get the mail without smearing SPF 55 sunscreen over your exposed skin." Done! Much of the damage was inflicted long ago, and it never really goes away. But at least I've fended off any new damage in recent years.

3) I finally started getting an annual physical exam. A good friend and former boss of mine scared me to death when he was about 40, and I was in my 20s. He was telling the tale of the prostate exam portion of getting a physical, and he made it sound like torture.

I never forgot that, and adopted (again) the stubborn male philosophy of, "If it ain't broke, don't fix it." My dad was among many who would say, "If you go to the doctor when you're not sick, they'll find something wrong with you anyway." So unless I was deathly ill with a stomach virus, I stayed out of doctors' offices. Finally, I gave in to spousal pressure, and made the annual date with the doctor. Thankfully, the uncomfortable exam I had dreaded wasn't so bad after all. It only lasts a few seconds. And the good doctor has monitored my once-high cholesterol levels, and introduced me to the delightful colonoscopy. That procedure deserves a story of its own, which you may read immediately following this one.

4) I finally visited a sleep center. Throughout our marriage, Cindy often expressed amazement I was still alive each

morning, after enduring sleepless nights of my high-decibel snoring, the rattle frequently interrupted by gasping for breath. Of course, I had no idea this was happening. All I knew was, I would awaken bone-tired, like I had worked in a cotton field all night. I would often lumber out of the bed wondering why I was so exhausted. Eventually I'd snap out of it, but mornings were not pleasant. I signed up for a sleep test, with all the sticky electrodes and uncomfortable gear making it darn near impossible to sleep. But evidently, the doctor acquired enough data and video evidence to prove that I had sleep apnea. The solution: a lovely C-PAP device that covers your nose, keeping your airways open.

There was another happy ending. Almost immediately, I slept better, stopped snoring, and have since felt great when I wake up each day.

Nothing I've written here is revolutionary, or considered a recent medical breakthrough. Certainly, I've been blessed to work for a good employer with a health insurance plan that allows me to make regular doctor visits and undergo these treatments. I wish everyone could do the same with no hassle or financial worries. But if anyone reads this, and is able and willing to get their allergies under control, regular physical exams (and if appropriate, colonoscopies), skin cancer screening or sleep apnea testing, it might make their life better too.

I Got a Colonoscopy: Now, That's What I Call a Blast

Due to some family history, I'm in the "every five years" category for colonoscopies. As you may know, colorectal cancer—cancer of the colon or rectum—is the second-leading killer in the United States, according to the Centers for Disease Control and Prevention. Removing precancerous growths spotted during a colonoscopy can cut the risk of dying from colon cancer in half. More than 95 percent of tumors are detected during a colonoscopy. Quite honestly, had my family doctor not made the first appointment for me about ten years ago, I would have never gone to the trouble.

When I shared a few Facebook comments about my colonoscopy, I was surprised by the number of people who are squeamish about it. Although it is strongly recommended for adults 50 and over (and younger folks with a family history of colon cancer), people hear the horror stories about an all-nighter on the john, the nasty liquid mixture you have to guzzle, and being probed from behind by total strangers. So they just say no. Or they say, "I'll get around to it, someday."

Allow me to list some random observations that may help, should you decide to take the plunge (*there I go again*).

1) If your procedure is scheduled for say, Thursday morning, start tapering off on your meals around Monday. Lighten up on your portions a little bit. Let's just say by Wednesday night, the more is not the merrier. You'll thank me later.

2) The "nasty liquid mixture" you've been hearing about is somewhat outdated. Most doctors now prescribe a clean-out potion that isn't all that bad. You can either mix it with clear Gatorade, or take tablets as I did (with LOTS

of clear liquid), with no taste at all. The end result is the same, but getting there isn't as bad as you've heard. Just don't stray too far from the bathroom for a few hours. If you go out to get the mail, you might soon be running in with an express delivery.

(That reminds me of a story from my first colonoscopy. During one of my many visits to the bathroom the night before the procedure, I looked at the bottle of liquid laxative I was chugging. It was called "Go Litely." On the floor was a bottle of bathroom cleanser, labeled "KaBoom." I remember thinking "KaBoom" would have been a more appropriate name for the laxative.)

3) Schedule your appointment first thing in the morning. That way, you do the dirty work starting at 5 p.m. the day before, sleep from about 12:30 to 5:30 a.m., and they do the deed around 7 a.m. The anesthesiologist works his magic, you drift off into dreamland, and the next thing you know you're sipping a cold drink and they send you on your way. You never feel a thing.

Full disclosure: in the immediate aftermath, there's a little, uh, "gas" involved, if you get my drift, and I'm afraid several innocent bystanders did.

You're home by 8:30 a.m. You sleep it off for a few hours, and then: chow time. What can you eat? Anything you want.

My lovely wife warmed up a great meal for my post-colonoscopy homecoming. It had served as dinner for her and my son while I was otherwise occupied the night before. It was the forbidden feast while I was on the all-liquid, in-and-out diet. I was most envious at the time, but I looked at it as my eventual reward for not whining about it.

By the way, I'm happy to report a successful outcome *(that's enough)*. When the doctor inserted a thin, flexible colonoscope up into its intended target area, the tiny camera sent images back to Earth that showed no polyps, no problems, not even that piece of gum I swallowed when I was in 2nd grade. I got to hear those magic words: "We'll see you back here in five years. Now go get something to eat!"

If you are reading this, and you are able and willing to get your allergies under control, to undergo regular physical exams (including colonoscopy, if appropriate), and to have skin cancer screening or sleep apnea testing, it might make your life better too.

CHAPTER 5:

Name Dropping

Chattanooga's Mr. Belding and *Saved by the Bell*

Longtime Chattanooga radio personality Garry Mac interviewing Dennis Haskins, 1980

The same duo, still having fun thirty years later

Every now and then, you'll hear someone say, "If you ever make it to Hollywood, don't forget your friends!" Well, Dennis Haskins made it to Hollywood more than thirty years ago, and he hasn't forgotten us. The Chattanooga native, a proud alumnus of Notre Dame High School and the University of Tennessee at Chattanooga (UTC) is a frequent visitor to his hometown, and he always makes us smile.

Prior to his acting career, Dennis managed and promoted several acts in the 1970s, including Overland Express.

Dennis first got national attention as "King of the Don't Blinks," as in, don't blink or you'll miss him. He was often cast in bit parts, including the first episode of "Dukes of Hazzard," playing a long-haired, mouthy rascal who got a little too close to Daisy Duke. Soon he was turning up in various TV shows, but rarely for more than a minute or so. That all changed in 1988 when he was hired to play the principal in a Saturday morning sitcom called "Good Morning Miss Bliss," which soon morphed into "Saved by the Bell." NBC picked up the show, and it's been on TV ever since. You can bet that somewhere in the world, one of those reruns is on the air.

As Principal Richard Belding, Dennis played the well-meaning, but often befuddled authority figure at Bayside High School. Zack, Slater, Screech, Jessie, Lisa and Kelly were always up to something, and Mr. Belding was there to smooth things out. On more than one occasion, the gang would try to sneak something past him, usually resulting in Mr. Belding exclaiming, "Hey, hey, hey, hey, hey . . . WHAT is going ON here?" Things always worked out fine, and kids across America wished they had a principal who was that cool.

I got to know Dennis pretty well while he was filming the show, and have a lot of great memories from those years. Each

Christmas he would come back to Chattanooga to visit his family (in fact, he had a framed picture of them in his TV principal's office). He would always ask me to line up a visit to Children's Hospital. The kids were thrilled to see a genuine TV star, and he was even happier to pose for pictures and sign autographs.

In 1992, I talked my boss into flying a news photographer and me to Los Angeles to do some behind-the-scenes stories on Dennis and his show, and we had a great time. The cast members and producers couldn't have been nicer, despite the fact they were cranking out shows one after another, with little time to socialize. We had a lot of laughs doing these stories, and they are still being viewed on my YouTube channel.

After the original kids "graduated," there were several sequels: The College Years, The New Class and others. New cast members floated in and out, but Mr. Belding was the one constant, and Dennis remains happily attached to the show today.

When Dennis visits Chattanooga, several of my younger coworkers eagerly line up for selfies, and Dennis never disappoints. He's always approachable, and is genuinely grateful for the fame and friendships he's gained over the years.

In recent years, he's appeared in "How I Met Your Mother," "Mad Men," "Tonight with Jimmy Fallon" and Seth MacFarlane's "A Million Ways to Die in the West."

Dennis is a huge fan of the UTC Mocs, often showing up at games, or tweeting about their big wins. His parents have both passed away in recent years, but he still comes back to Chattanooga during the holidays to reunite with his old friends from radio, TV, music and sports. We call our annual luncheon "A Very Dennis Christmas," because it just seems right.

In 2015, Dennis graduated from UTC, with a Bachelor's degree in Theater. What a great milestone for him, at the age of 65. Please don't tell the kids from "Saved by the Bell" that Mr. Belding was a few credits shy of his diploma, for all those years.

Sure, they thought he was a few bricks shy of a load, but that's another story.

Dennis will always be part of our family, and we enjoy keeping up with him on both the small screen and the big screen.

Where Were You When Elvis Died?

On August 16, 1977, our world was rocked by the death of the man who had been rocking our world. It was big news when Elvis Presley died suddenly at the age of 42, unless you were Walter Cronkite. The "CBS Evening News" didn't consider Elvis's death to be the lead story that night. (Good old NBC did, thank you very much. Or as Elvis would have said, "thankyouverymuch.")

During that time, I worked in the family store by day, attended college by night, and worked at WGOW in Chattanooga on Saturdays. The 16th was a Tuesday, and I had a report to write for a class that night. I was working on it at 4:30 that afternoon with "The Brady Bunch" in the background. Why? I don't know. Maybe Marcia Brady helped me stay awake while I was studying (yawn) business management.

Channel 9 anchorman Bob Johnson interrupted the Bradys, with a voice-over report. There was no video, just a "News Bulletin" slide on the screen. I had the volume on low, so I missed the first part. By the time I started listening, all I heard was that someone had died at Baptist Hospital in Memphis. Who, in Tennessee was so important that they rated a news bulletin at 4:45 p.m.? (In those days, the local news didn't come on until 6:00). I had a paper to write, so I kept going. A few minutes later, Bob's voice came back on, and again, I only heard the last few words.

My curiosity got the best of me, so I turned on the radio. It was set on WGOW, and they were playing an Elvis song. I switched to WFLI, and they too were playing an Elvis song. This was no coincidence, I thought.

Soon, the sad news was confirmed. Elvis was too young to die; he was only 42. Sure, he was overweight. But that was just a phase, we thought. He gains it, he loses it, like many of us do. He had just appeared in concert in Huntsville a few months before. My sister Elaine, always an Elvis fan, had invited me to go. I passed, for some reason or other. "I'll catch him next time," I said, because there's always a next time. Not this time. I never got to see Elvis, and have regretted it ever since.

As the news spread, the huge reaction surprised even me. I was little when President John F. Kennedy was assassinated, but the public outpouring of grief made a huge impression. A few years later, the violent deaths of Martin Luther King and Bobby Kennedy were equally shocking. All of them, gone in an instant, far too young.

And now Elvis was gone. It may be hard for today's kids to understand, but in the pre-Internet/smartphone era, we had TV, movies and radio. Period. Elvis dominated them all just as baby-boomers were coming of age. Before my time, he shook up the sleepy 1950s with his swiveling hips and rockabilly hits. In the 1960s, he was overshadowed on the radio by the British Invasion, so he made movies. Late in the decade, he reinvented himself with a dynamic TV special and began paying more attention to his music, resulting in some of his best songs ever. He recorded "Suspicious Minds," "Kentucky Rain" and "Burning Love," to name a few.

Then, we were told he had become dependent on all kinds of drugs. His outfits were too tight, and his live shows were sloppy. He became the butt of jokes. Suddenly, he was gone. America, especially the under-35 generation, mourned. One of our local newspapers, with a very conservative viewpoint, rarely mentioned Elvis during his lifetime. But sensing a financial windfall, they ran special "Sunday Elvis" sections for several weeks after his death. Even now, RCA is still releasing "new" Elvis music, unearthed and remixed from deep in their vaults.

Although I was a little young to have been an original Elvis fan, I understood his appeal. I played his songs on the radio, and still enjoy many of them today. Other music legends who left us at a young age, like Michael Jackson, John Lennon, and Whitney Houston, certainly left their mark. But he may have been the most original, and apparently he had the biggest impact. Otherwise, why would so many still be imitating him today?

Miracle Man Tommy Jett and
the Healing Power of Rock 'n Roll

On the air with everybody's close personal friend, Tommy Jett, in 2011

On May 4, 2013, a silver-haired man with a ring on every finger stepped up to the podium at the Tennessee Radio Hall of Fame banquet. The newly inducted deejay thanked his family, his listeners, his God, and his "close personal friends." Thankfully, he didn't name each of them because it would have taken all night.

In a career spanning more than a half-century, Tommy Jett has amassed a following like few others. Starting at WFLI (AM 1070) in Chattanooga, Tommy provided the soundtrack to the Baby Boomer generation. In 2015 "TJ the DJ" celebrated the publication of his biography, an event he never thought he would live to see.

Tommy's was one of the first rock 'n roll voices I heard on the transistor radio of my youth. It soon became obvious to me that no one loved his job, or his listeners more than Tommy.

When I got into radio and began working at WFLI, we would have lunch now and then, and I would sit back and watch as his fans stopped and stared at him. With his sharp suits, big sunglasses, and a ring on every finger, he stood out in a crowd. They would yell his catch-phrase, "Hey now, you're TJ the DJ!" He took time to speak to every one of them.

On April 18, 2012, the longtime diabetic, then 71, lost consciousness while driving along a rural north Georgia road. His car went airborne, flipping a half-dozen times before landing in a ditch. Emergency workers spent the next four hours removing Tommy from the wreckage, using the "Jaws of Life." Walker County Deputy Bruce Coker led the rescue effort. "I thought there was no way we could get him out alive," Coker said later.

Yet within days, Tommy was holding court in his hospital room, recovering from neck surgery. He was determined to attend his annual Entertainers Reunion, scheduled in May. As Tommy said, "If I'm above ground, I'll be there." He made that date, and even emceed the Riverbend Festival in June. But he was getting weaker by the day, losing weight rapidly. The once robust rock-and-roller had lost his appetite.

It all came to a head in late June. His wife Charlene, who had tried mightily to get him to eat, called 911. He had lapsed into a coma. He was rushed to a Chattanooga hospital, and friends started spreading the word: this didn't look good.

On Sunday, July 1st, the phone calls went out. "If you want to see Tommy Jett alive, you'd better hurry." He was being kept alive on a respirator, and doctors told Charlene the bad news: "He will never get better." That afternoon, she told friends she was beginning to accept the inevitable. By morning, family members were called in to say goodbye. Funeral arrangements were made, a church was chosen, and pallbearers were notified.

What happened next has yet to be explained, scientifically anyway. Some longtime radio friends hatched an idea. Yes,

Tommy was lying in a hospital bed, lifeless. But what did Tommy enjoy more than anything else? Being on the radio, playing the hits. So the radio guys got a boom box, loaded in some CD recordings of Tommy's WFLI "Night Train" shows from the 1960s, and cranked it up at the head of Tommy's bed. When one disc ran out, a new one was put in. Elvis, the Supremes, the Beatles, all introduced by Tommy. It sounded just as it had aired on the radio fifty years earlier.

Monday morning arrived, and to everyone's surprise, doctors did not "pull the plug." They told the family that Tommy had shown slight signs of improvement. Tommy was still in a deep sleep, as the music played on. "Come on and be my little good luck charm," Elvis crooned. Tommy's lively voice would interrupt between songs: "Nineteen minutes after midnight, you're movin' and groovin', with Super-Jett, your ever-lovin' leader!"

The next day, Tommy began to move his fingers just a bit. By Wednesday, he was blinking his eyes. Later that day his eyes began following the movements of his grandchildren in the hospital room. Message received: Tommy wasn't ready to "check out" just yet.

By Friday, five days after his pals came by to say goodbye, they witnessed what can only be described as a miracle. There was Tommy, now able to speak, laugh, and express his thanks. Did he hear the music during his deep sleep? No one, not even Tommy can be sure. But it certainly didn't hurt. And if anyone wants to attach a little healing power to the sounds of rock and roll, so be it. His wife Charlene said, "When the #1 doctor, God stepped in and said it is not time yet, Tommy woke up. We give much credit to the doctors, but Tommy and I know the real reason he is here is God."

Tommy can't hide a smile when it's suggested that maybe rock and roll had something to do with his amazing recovery. "There's nothing like music," he says. "It's been a big part of my whole life." As for me, I'm telling my family to keep some Tommy Jett CDs handy. If I'm ever the subject of those serious hospital conversations, crank up "TJ the DJ" for me. That'll make me want to stick around a while longer too.

Memories of Jackie and Tojo

Those of us who grew up watching local TV in the "baby boomer era" surely remember these names: Jackie and Tojo.

Jackie Fargo was one of our first TV superstars. Yes, we had cowboys, but they were on film and lived far away. We had baseball and football stars, but they rarely set foot in these parts. It was a pleasure then, to tune in "Live Wrestling" Saturday afternoons on Chattanooga's local TV channels, because there was a good chance that Jackie would be trading one-liners with ringleader/emcee Harry Thornton.

Jackie Fargo in the 1960s

Early in his career, Jackie (born Henry Faggart in North Carolina) started as a villain. A wrestler named Don Kalt played
Jackie's brother, and as a tag team, they would wreak havoc on
the good guys. By the 1960s, Jackie had evidently seen the light,
and turned into a good guy with just a hint of mischief. His usual
opponents were introduced as Japanese or German, and we
fans were happy to see Jackie cheat a little to pay them back for
World War II. The wrestler who played "Don Fargo" later took
on another identity, so Jackie's real brother Sonny was pressed
into service as his tag-team partner.

Thornton, always the master promoter, knew a goldmine
when he saw it. Every year or so, he saw to it that Jackie would
have a bitter feud with either the Germans or the Japanese.
Quite often, Jackie's foe was the evil Tojo Yamamoto. Tojo's
real name, by the way, was Harold Watanabe. He was born in
Hawaii. But we wanted him to be Japanese, and Thornton said
that he was. That was good enough for me.

Tojo Yamamoto (top, with Yoshino Sato) in the 1960s

Tojo was a scowling, menacing presence. For several consecutive Saturdays, Jackie would appear on the Chattanooga wrestling show for a friendly interview with Harry to promote an upcoming appearance, or a favorite charity. Then out of nowhere, Tojo would emerge, waging a sneak attack on Jackie with one of his wooden shoes. Jackie, caught by surprise, would wipe away blood (or something that looked like it) and vow revenge.

For weeks at a time, the live wrestling show would go something like this: Jackie would pummel Tojo, pin him to the mat, and the referee would pound the canvas, yelling, "One! Two!" and then Tojo would miraculously rise up and start pounding away on Jackie. He would pin the hero to the mat, and again the referee would start the count: "One! Two!" and somehow Jackie would spring forward. This sequence would repeat a few times until about 5:55 p.m., when a bell would ring and Harry Thornton would announce, "Stop the match, we're out of time!"

Kids like me could be heard yelling, "No! No! Jackie's about to win, you can't stop now!" Harry would explain that they couldn't go past the time limit due to federal law, or whatever, but I later figured out what he was up to.

Harry would set up a grudge match between the two combatants, but it would not be shown on TV. No sir, this match was so big, it would have to be staged in front of 5,000 screaming fans at Memorial Auditorium, all of whom were more than willing to cough up the cash to see how it played out. Harry was no fool. Kids throughout the region ran to their parents, begging and pleading for tickets to this major event.

Those fortunate enough to attend saw a longer version of the weekly TV slugfest. The rest of us would have to depend on newspaper accounts or friends who had attended. Otherwise, we'd have to wait until the next Saturday when Harry would report the outcome. Sadly, there were none of the video highlights we take for granted today.

As the years went by, Jackie's Chattanooga appearances became less frequent. He was in demand in larger cities like Memphis, Nashville, Atlanta and Birmingham. But his fans will always remember his charismatic personality and "The Fargo Strut," his signature stride after defeating a rival. It was often imitated by his adoring 10-year-old fans.

As I got a little older, my big-city friends revealed a shocking secret. After the matches at Memorial Auditorium, they said, Jackie, Tojo, and the other wrestlers would go out to eat. In fact, they shared the same table at the Old South Restaurant. "That's impossible," I would reply. "They hate each other!" No, they would assure me, these guys understood their roles, and how not to seriously hurt each other. They traveled together, they roomed together, and they ate together. For me, this finally solved the mystery of how wrestlers could seemingly beat the daylights out of each other every night, while boxers like Muhammad Ali would take several months between matches. I had not been able to understand why boxers got so much attention, when they only fought three or four times a year.

Still, the passion they inspired was fierce. Saturday wrestling was my original Must-See-TV, and I wasn't alone. Jackie and his fellow grapplers inspired many of us to roll around on the playground in our own elementary role-playing.

A few years ago, I looked up Jackie in a Google search, and learned that he was living his retirement years in North Carolina, still making a few personal appearances, enjoying his fame and welcoming his fans. North Carolina's not that far away, I thought. One of these days, I'll track down his phone number, make a visit and tell him how much I appreciated his style and showmanship. I'd say it couldn't have been easy, choreographed or not, to take those hits, make those falls and flips, and deal with those in-your-face fans. I'd thank him for entertaining folks from 4 to 104, getting their minds off their own problems for an hour or two each week. And I would tell him how rich someone would be, if they had figured out a way to videotape and re-sell those 1960s wrestling shows decades later. At the time, they had no way of knowing their weekly slugfests would be in demand in the 21st century.

Sadly, I waited too late. Jackie died in 2013, just before his 83rd birthday. I hope that somewhere, in that big Southern diner in the sky, Jackie, Tojo, Harry and the others are having some laughs as they swap stories about those good times and wild nights in the wrestling ring.

Remembering the March of Dimes Telerama

Autograph card for Chattanooga's first March of Dimes Telerama, 1967

It seems hard to believe now, but for 11 years (1967-77), Chattanooga viewers watched a 19-hour annual telethon, from 11:00 p.m. Saturday to 6:00 p.m. Sunday, for the March of Dimes. Broadcast live from first the Tivoli Theater, and later the Memorial Auditorium, the stage was filled with celebrities, and the technical gear was operated by crews from all three local TV stations. Once a year, competition was put aside for a common goal: the battle against birth defects.

The March of Dimes *Telerama* was held each January, usually hosted by Roy Morris Roy was a popular TV personality who also acted and sang in Little Theater productions, so he was quite capable of leading a marathon TV production.

Similar March of Dimes telethons were broadcast by stations nationwide beginning in the early 1960s, all following the same format. Local singers and bands were recruited to perform, because 19 hours is a lot of time to fill. National celebrities provided some star power. With only three networks on the air, there weren't many stars to go around, but a surprising number of them volunteered their time. James Arness and Dennis Weaver from *Gunsmoke*, Fess Parker and Ed Ames from *Daniel Boone*, and Max Baer and Irene Ryan from *The Beverly Hillbillies* made the rounds from Pittsburgh, to Charlotte, to Knoxville, Seattle and beyond to help the March of Dimes. Some, like Weaver, Parker, and Ames could sing on the shows. Others would simply appear on stage, joke around with the hosts, and help answer the phones. Fans who attended the shows often got autographs from the stars.

I made my first TV appearance on a Telerama. The producers would ask local radio personalities to man the pledge table, reading the challenges that had been phoned in. This was a thrill for me, then a teenage disc jockey. When the regular host took a wee-hours break, someone signaled for me to go on stage and introduce a local singing group. Sure, it was 3:30 a.m., but I was on TV! A couple of hours later, the real host re-emerged, and I slithered back into obscurity.

Perhaps the biggest star to appear was Michael Landon in 1967. His western series, *Bonanza*, was riding high in the ratings, and everybody loved "Little Joe." Landon stayed busy posing for pictures, signing autographs, and making a tearful (and effective) plea for viewers to donate.

Each year, we would anxiously await the announcement of the next Telerama stars. The producers tried to top themselves each year. In 1968, Leonard Nimoy was the headliner. That was a bit of a letdown after Landon the year before. It sounds strange now, but *Star Trek* wasn't that popular when it originally aired on NBC, so an appearance by "Mr. Spock" didn't create much excitement at the time. Sharing the bill with Nimoy were James Drury of *The Virginian*, "King of the Road" singer Roger Miller, and country comedian Minnie Pearl, so collectively there were plenty of stars.

In the years to come, guests included David Canary of *Bonanza*; *Hee Haw* stars Roy Clark, Gunilla Hutton, and Roni Stoneman; *Laugh-In* cast member Richard Dawson, Peter Marshall of *Hollywood Squares*, Anson Williams of *Happy Days*, Robert Reed of *The Brady Bunch*, Donna Douglas of *The Beverly Hillbillies*, and singer Crystal Gayle.

Local telethons eventually faded out, giving way to national extravaganzas like Jerry Lewis's annual Muscular Dystrophy Telethon, which is now also a thing of the past. But for more than a decade, viewers were treated to an annual gathering of national talent that is still remembered fondly today.

Miss Marcia in the Morning

Chattanooga's sweetheart, "Miss Marcia," in the 1960s

Marcia Kling retired from Chattanooga's WTVC Channel 9 on May 30, 2013. I am honored to share my love for "Miss Marcia" with you.

Our relationship began, unbeknownst to her, when I was a wee lad. I hadn't even started first grade. You see, in ancient times we didn't have Head Start or pre-K, and in rural Alabama we didn't have kindergarten. If you were lucky (as was I), you had parents or older siblings who would teach you the basics before you started school. Still, they couldn't cover everything. So it fell to Miss Marcia to teach me how to tie my shoes, mind my manners and tell time. Oh yes, tell time. Thanks to her, I learned when the big hand was on the 12, and the little hand was on the 9, it was 9 o'clock: "Funtime," which just happened to be the name of her show.

Miss Marcia's morning kiddie show featured games and songs with local children in the studio (lucky them!). She would often talk about her own son, John David (even luckier!). The highlight of each day was when she sang her own "Happy Birthday" song. As Chattanooga area baby boomers know, this wasn't the traditional birthday song. It was Miss Marcia's version, featuring high notes most of us could never hope to reach. That didn't keep us from trying, but we learned quickly that Miss Marcia was often imitated but never duplicated.

A New York native, she came to Maryville, Tennessee for her education in the late 1950s, moving to Chattanooga a few years later. She first took a job at a church, then as a school teacher. In 1962, the original host of WTVC's *Romper Room* left the show, and Marcia was recruited to try out. She was an immediate hit, and a year later the show was renamed *Funtime*, enduring for fifteen years.

Unfortunately, there were some rough spots along the way. In the early 1970s, Miss Marcia was diagnosed with oral cancer. Her absence was noticeable to her young audience. WTVC knew she was irreplaceable. Rather than try to come up with an interim host, the station ran cartoons during her illness. Entertaining, yes, but educational, no. Thankfully, she was back at the piano several months later.

What few people knew at the time was, this was no ordinary illness, the kind where you just need a few months of rest and recuperation. Miss Marcia had to learn to speak again, from word one. This extraordinary hostess, teacher and entertainer, who had spoken so clearly and sang so beautifully, worked hard to return to this most visible job.

She remained at WTVC after the children's show ended, and continued to produce and host shows for slightly older kids (*Nifty Nine*) and in later years, for senior adults (*Lifewatch*).

I finally got to meet my childhood sweetheart as an adult. One day at the mall, I was with Chris and Vince, who were about five and two at the time. I saw Miss Marcia, and said, "Guys, you've got to meet this lady! I grew up watching her on TV!" She gave me a hug, and I introduced the boys to her. She made the appropriate fuss over them. I didn't see her in person again until about five years later, and this time I was by myself. "Hi, Miss Marcia," I said. "Well, hello David, how are you?" she responded. "And how are those fine boys of yours, Chris and Vince?" As I've told and retold that story over the years, I've learned, that my experience was not uncommon. She remembers names like no one else. You can call it a gift, but I call it being thoughtful and caring.

When my previous book was published in 2011, I wanted to attract a crowd at my first book signing at Chattanooga's Northgate Mall. I figured I'd have a better chance of reaching that goal if I invited the two most famous people in the book to accompany me. Radio legend Luther Masingill quickly accepted, and Miss Marcia graciously did the same. (I wanted to call the event *Two and a Half Celebrities*, but somebody nixed that idea.) Mission accomplished: Chattanooga's two most famous faces drew quite a crowd.

I'm glad that Miss Marcia stepped away from the daily grind in good health, and has continued her impressive record of helping every charity that comes her way. I don't have many regrets about my career, but here's one of them: I never got to work with her on a daily basis. Unlike my friends Bill Race, Darrell Patterson and Bob Johnson, I didn't get that daily dose of Miss Marcia sunshine in person. I should point out however, that when I was little, I thought she could see me through the TV camera. I later told her that, and she laughed and said, "Oh yes, I could see you." She was joking. I hope.

A final thought: for some odd reason Tennessee, with its various Halls of Fame, has not established a Broadcasting Hall of Fame. We now have a Radio Hall of Fame, but there isn't one that recognizes legendary television personalities. We need to make that happen. When we do, this all-time great TV teacher, who worked fifty-one years at the same TV station should be among the first honorees.

After School with Bob Brandy

The Original Marshmallow Sandwich

Compliments of

Chattanooga Bakeries, Inc.

Watch Bob and Ingrid on the Bob Brandy Show—
4:30-5:30 Daily on Channel 9, WTVC

MOON PIE

Promo card for Ingrid and Bob Brandy, 1960s

Whenever you meet a "baby boomer" from the Chattanooga area, a few questions always come up. "Where did you go to school?" "Remember all that air pollution?" And, this one: "Were you ever on the *Bob Brandy Show*?"

Back in the 1960s, we all loved singing cowboys. In the grand tradition of Roy Rogers and Gene Autry, our Chattanooga singing cowboy had legions of fans. Bob Brandy (shortened from Brandenburg) was one of WTVC Channel 9's first hires. When the station was preparing for its first broadcast from Signal Mountain, the owners knew they would be competing with the already-established WDEF Channel 12 (CBS) and

WRGP Channel 3 (NBC). It was February 1958, and the Channel 9 area license had been transferred from Rome, Georgia to Chattanooga. WTVC was affiliating with the third-place ABC network, so this new station would need someone to get the city's attention.

Enter Bob Brandy. He had started a kids' show in Columbus, Georgia a year earlier, and had developed a strong following. Along with his wife Ingrid, and his horse Rebel, Bob welcomed scout troops and school groups. Sponsors furnished prizes to give away, and Bob provided the fun and games. In the early days of live TV, Bob Brandy faced the camera for an hour each afternoon as the kids got home from school.

Bob's show soon found an eager audience. The other channels had also aired kids shows (Channel 12's *Mr. Chickaroonie* and Channel 3's *Alex and Elmer* are well-remembered), but they had faded by the early 1960s. Sponsors like Chattanooga Bakery (Moon Pie) and McKee Bakery (Little Debbie snacks) quickly saw the benefits of Bob giving away their goodies to kids who sat on Rebel and threw a ball into a barrel. When Bob needed a break, he'd show a Three Stooges comedy or a Popeye cartoon. Once or twice during the show, the Bob Brandy Trio would perform a cowboy song.

Bob's wife Ingrid, with a thick German accent and tightly-coiffed blond hair, would help interview the kids. One widely quoted story, which was apparently seen by everyone in the Tennessee Valley, recalls a day in which some mischievous 10-year-old boys were laughing uncontrollably while Bob was trying to talk. He wanted to find out what was going on, so he asked them what was so funny. One kid looked right into the camera and said, "Charlie farted!" You can't beat live television.

My friend Gary Wordlaw got his first job at WTVC, working on the studio crew. He told me that Bob's show ended five minutes before the local news came on, from the same studio.

He remembers scooping and mopping some of Rebel's drop-pings, under the hot lights, just moments before the anchorman started reading the news. Gary stayed in the TV business for forty years, but thanks to Rebel, his first job made a really strong impression.

Those of us who never got to be on Bob's show were often fortunate enough to see him in our hometown. On Saturdays, Bob took his show on the road, complete with Rebel, the musicians and the prizes. When they visited Bryant Junior High School, I think the whole community showed up.

All good things must come to an end, so Bob's show was eventually taken off the weekday schedule. It bounced around on weekends for a couple of years until Bob decided to sing "Happy Trails" once and for all.

Bob continued his day job, selling commercials for WTVC, eventually becoming the station's sales manager. It turns out Bob was a top TV ad salesman through the show's entire run, no doubt using his fame to his advantage. I mean, who wouldn't want to buy some time on the *Bob Brandy Show*? For the next thirty years, until his death in 2003 at the age of 72, Bob stayed loyal to WTVC. Even after retirement, he was a consultant for the station.

I got to know Bob a little bit late in his life. He was not in good health, but he always smiled when someone told him they grew up with him. It brought back memories of a more inno-cent time. These days, the mere mention of his name brings a smile to those who tuned in each afternoon. I think he'd like that.

Watching Mort Lloyd on the News

Mort Lloyd reporting election results in 1964

I never got to meet Mort Lloyd, although he was in my living room every day for years. He was Chattanooga's most-watched TV news anchorman for twenty years. He switched channels a couple of times, and his loyal viewers always followed him. He died in a plane crash on August 20, 1974, setting off my list of "What If?" questions.

What if he had decided to stay in TV? By 1974, he had tired of the daily TV grind. Twenty years earlier, at the age of 23, the Shelbyville, Tennessee native was hired by WDEF Channel 12 to be its first news anchor the day it signed on the air. At that time, when radio was still king, TV announcers were hired primarily for their voices, and no one's voice was deeper than

Mort's. His first radio job was at WHAL in his hometown, before making it big at WSIX in Nashville. When he took the WDEF-TV job, Mort's hair was already thinning, and he decided to shave his head, a rarity in television. His distinctive appearance and bass voice caught on with viewers.

In 1956, Channel 3 (then WRGP-TV) signed on, also offering a nightly newscast. By 1958, Channel 3 was making no progress in the ratings against Mort, so they lured him away from Channel 12. It was a bold move, and Channel 3 made a big splash with Mort's hire, putting billboards all over town. His Channel 3 newscast shot to the top of the ratings and remained there for twelve years.

In 1970, Channel 12's manager decided his station had been in second place long enough, so he offered Mort enough cash to come back to his old station. Mort accepted the offer, under the conditions that the news department would be expanded, and that his longtime weatherman John Gray would come over from Channel 3 too. History repeated itself, as Mort's viewers again loyally followed him, putting Mort and "the TV-12 Professionals" on top of the ratings.

It was obvious from the beginning: no one else looked like Mort, and no one else sounded like Mort. Unfortunately, no known video exists of Mort's live newscasts. Back then, video tape was expensive, so the newscasts were broadcast live, and none were saved. There are a few snippets of audio that were preserved, and they're among the most popular items on my YouTube channel. Unlike today's short-attention span, bang-bang newscasts, Mort worked in a three-channel universe. His audience was comparatively captive in the pre-remote control era, so he read the news slowly, pronouncing each precious syllable in his deliberate, distinctive style: "Police are searching . . .

for two armed bandits . . . said to be in the . . . Brainerd . . . area."

With his shaved head and deeper-than-deep voice, he was
other-worldly to me. In fact, the station's set designer wisely
placed a globe, hanging from a string, next to his bald dome. As
a kid, I was mesmerized. With the head, the voice, and planet
Earth right there on my black-and-white TV, Mort Lloyd could
just as well have been from another planet. He sure didn't sound
like anyone I knew!

By 1974, Mort was dissatisfied with what was going on in
Washington. Richard Nixon was in the White House, and Re-
publicans were facing a tough mid-term election year. Incumbent GOP 3rd Dist. Rep. Lamar Baker was in his second term,
and Mort decided to seek the office as a Democrat. He was 43
years old. Had he decided to stay in TV, he could have surely
made a comfortable living for decades to come. Instead, he took
a leave of absence from the news desk, and tested the political
waters.

In early August, he won the Democratic primary, capturing
60 percent of the vote against two opponents. Heading into the
November general election, he was considered the favorite
against Rep. Baker. Mort's TV persona had made him a familiar
face, and Baker was not a particularly charismatic Congressman.
With the stench of Nixon's Watergate scandal still fresh in vot-
ers' minds, it was not a good time to be a Republican candidate.

On August 20, 1974, Mort decided to fly his 1946 Swift air-
plane to Shelbyville, Tennessee to visit his parents. He was a
veteran pilot, and had flown his plane to destinations near and
far. As far back as 1958, when a Chattanooga judge faced an
impeachment trial in Nashville, Mort flew to the state capital
each morning, returning to report the story on the Channel 3
evening newscast.

He took off, flying solo from Chattanooga that morning shortly after 11:00 a.m. He never made it to Shelbyville.

Thirty minutes into his flight, a blade broke loose from the propeller assembly, throwing the engine off balance. The engine shook loose from its mount, and the plane spun out of control. Witnesses saw the plane go down in a wooded field near Manchester. Mort was found slumped over in his seat.

What if he had lived? Political observers say he would have likely won the 3rd District Congressional seat. He was young, popular, and in good health.

Mort's widow Marilyn told Democratic leaders she wanted to run for the seat in the November election, despite formidable competition from two big names: Chattanooga developer Franklin Haney and Oak Ridge banker Jake Butcher. Both were wealthy, and both had recently run for governor, losing the Democratic nomination to Ray Blanton. Mrs. Lloyd had campaigned with her husband, and was a savvy businesswoman, having operated a radio station she and Mort owned in Dalton, Georgia. The party chose Mrs. Lloyd over Haney and Butcher, and she easily defeated Rep. Baker. She served ten terms before retiring from Congress in 1994.

We'll never know what Mort might have achieved in government. Would he have chosen to run for U.S. Senate, as many House members do? Would his popularity have spread statewide? What were his interests, and his causes? Would he have used his influence in constructive ways for TVA, the Chickamauga Lock, highways and health care? Or would he have become frustrated by Washington, and opted to return to television?

We will never know. Still, more than forty years after his sudden death, it's important to note that he made quite an impact on the Chattanooga area in his brief lifetime.

U.S. Rep. Marilyn Lloyd in 1976

Congresswoman Marilyn Lloyd became a frequent guest on my shows, and a good friend. Thrust in political life by tragedy, she would often lean in during commercials and say, "David, take it easy on me, you know I'm not a politician."

We would then open the phone lines, taking calls live on the air. Mrs. Lloyd ("Just call me Marilyn") had no idea what the callers would say, or what they would ask. Occasionally an angry caller would complain about a tax increase, or a reduction in Social Security benefits. She would hear them out, give them the best explanation she could, and then always end with a smile. The caller, having calmed down considerably, would say, "Thank you so much Mrs. Lloyd . . . I mean Marilyn!"

We would go to commercial, and I'd lean over to Marilyn and say, "And you say you're not a politician. Right." She never lost an election.

Ain't That Right, Miz Mull?

Print advertisement for Mull's Singing Convention *in the 1960s
(Rev. Mull's first initial and middle name are misspelled.)*

A friend reminded me that I left someone out of my "Chattanooga Radio and Television" book. Despite my efforts to include the most memorable faces and voices of the city's 90-plus year broadcast history, I wasn't able to include everyone. In some cases, photos were not available, and in other cases I simply used poor judgement. "How," my friend asked, "did you manage to leave out Mull's Singing Convention?" Good question. For about thirty years, the faces of Rev. J. Bazzel Mull and his wife, Elizabeth (Lady Mull), were about as familiar as anyone's.

The Mulls first brought Southern Gospel music to Chattanooga TV in 1956. At first, the Mulls did a nightly show, before settling into a Saturday noon time slot on WTVC from 1960 until 1975, in glorious black and white. When the Chattanooga telecasts ended, the Mulls continued their show in their home base of Knoxville as long as they were physically able to go to the studio.

J. Bazzel, blind since a childhood accident at the age of 11 months, was best known for his raspy voice, and a frequent question to his wife that became a local catch-phrase: "Ain't that right, Miz Mull?" "That's right!" she would cheerily reply. He wore thick, tinted glasses, and many viewers had no idea he was blind.

From Channel 9's studio, the Mulls would introduce live or filmed performances from the Speer Family, the Blackwood Brothers, the Chuck Wagon Gang, and the LeFevres, to name a few. In addition, the Mulls would host multi-act concerts at Memorial Auditorium. They also sold truckloads of records and song books. At their peak, they presented 75 concerts, primarily in the Southeast, every year.

Today's young people might wonder how a weekend gospel music TV show had such a big impact. After all, in today's 400-channel universe, it's hard for anyone to get noticed. But in those days, with only three channels from which to choose, the Mulls were easy to find. They had a prime spot of TV real estate, between Saturday morning cartoons and college football games, so their weekly show was must-see TV for many, or just on in the background at the very least. Frankly, it was hard not to notice the voice of J. Bazzel Mull. We didn't know it at the time, but when the blind preacher would get carried away and lose track of time, "Lady Mull" would pinch his leg under the desk to let him know it was time to introduce the next group.

Chattanooga TV old-timers still chuckle about their J. Bazzel stories. The preacher loved a good joke, even when he was the subject. His blindness led to some (hopefully) good-natured pranks. One former Channel 9 crew member told me about the time Rev. Mull got wound up talking about a Bible issue. The fellows who had been listening tiptoed away, leaving the preacher talking to a hat rack for about five minutes. Another remembered an auditorium show in which the person who was supposed to lead him off the stage forgot to do so, leaving Rev. Mull standing awkwardly in front of a singing quartet for the better part of their song.

He didn't let his blindness keep him from his busy calling. Mrs. Mull, who drove him everywhere, faithfully read the Bible to him daily, and even late in life he had a photographic memory of every chapter and verse. The Mulls owned a Knoxville radio station, and his distinctive voice was also heard on powerful New Orleans station WWL with a nighttime signal that carried into several states. Long distance truckers were among the Mulls' biggest fans.

Both Mulls were inducted into the Southern Gospel Hall of Fame, and are credited with starting the careers of many acts that became household words. J. Bazzel passed away in 2006 at the age of 91, and Elizabeth passed away in 2012 at the age of 85. Their daughter Charlotte continued the show, but passed away the following year at 67.

The Mulls didn't make it into my first book, but I'm proud to include them in this one.

Whatever Happened to Chickamauga Charlie?

I've cited a few of my broadcasting influences, all of whom played a big part in my life. I knew I wanted to speak into a microphone, but much like the dog who chases the car, what would I do with the microphone if I ever caught it?

The answer came from an unlikely source. Thus begins the tale of one Chickamauga Charlie, AKA Chicky-Poo.

In the glory days of top-40 radio, disc jockeys were cheerful and chirpy, rattling off the song titles, the artists, the time and temperature, and the request line number. This was in direct contrast to the older radio guys who chatted a lot about their sponsors.

Chickamauga Charlie publicity photo, 1971

Then along came Chickamauga Charlie. He was a splash of cold water in the morning, and for me, a true wake-up call.

As an 8ᵗʰ grader, I had a daily routine while getting ready for school. The radio played an important part. One morning, I heard an unfamiliar voice on WGOW. This disc jockey is telling jokes, and making wisecracks about the mayor, the sheriff, and even the president. To top it off, he's breaking the cardinal rule of radio: he's making fun of the station's advertisers! If his goal was to get my attention, it was working.

I later found out that Ted Turner was behind all of this. Not quite a cable TV mogul at the time, Turner had attended school in Chattanooga, and owned some local businesses including WGOW. Although Turner was based in Atlanta, WGOW was an important piece of his budding empire, and it wasn't doing very well.

On his way home one afternoon, he heard a popular disc jockey on WQXI in Atlanta named Bob Todd. He wasn't like the others. He had attitude, humor, and an edgy style. What if, Turner wondered, he could get this guy to shake things up in the mornings on his Chattanooga station?

They made a deal, and soon Bob Todd became Chickamauga Charlie. For the first several months, he recorded his show in Atlanta, and sent the tapes on a bus to Chattanooga for over-night delivery. He began reading the Chattanooga newspapers to learn what the locals were talking about, so he could rip into the city's power structure. His act went over so well, he soon moved to Chattanooga to do his show live in WGOW's studio.

As he often said, he was "the disc jockey with no sacred cows." He wrote and delivered a daily satirical newscast ("The Little News") that poked fun at everybody who was anybody. One night, he made a surprise appearance at a business awards dinner, TV cameras in tow, and presented a "Polluter of the

Year" award to a local manufacturer. Now, that will get a city's attention.

Advertisers scrambled to get Chicky-Poo to read their commercials, with special instructions to make fun of the owner, giving him free rein to make their business stand out. He also cracked jokes about his co-workers, his newsman, and most memorably his station manager. Yes, he dared to make his own boss a daily punch line.

It was great radio, and I had never heard anything like it. One of my 8th grade teachers was Nathan Black, a cool guy who played drums in a band. He was about 25, and he also listened to Chicky-Poo. I enjoyed coming to school each morning, comparing notes with Mr. Black about the funny jokes and scathing social commentary we had heard on our way to school. (You can search for him on YouTube, and hear bits and pieces of his show.)

Each morning, Chicky would read a "Letter of the Day," which usually was something funny a listener had sent in. On the day he read my letter on the air, I was the star of North Sand Mountain High School.

Chickamauga Charlie was only in town for about three years. As suddenly as he had arrived on the local airwaves, he was gone.

Flash forward thirty years. No one in Chattanooga had seen or heard from Chicky since his departure. Having been his number one fan, I had borrowed, or perhaps stolen, some of his bits for my own radio shows on KZ-106. Occasionally someone would say, "That sounds like something Chicky would do," which was a real compliment.

Some people would inquire about his whereabouts, while others would share rumors that he had become a hippie living in a commune, or that he had moved to one state or another, and even that he had died. During those three decades, I would often wonder what had become of my radio idol.

Then came the Internet. Once it became apparent that almost anyone could be located, I set out to find Chickamauga Charlie. After a few false starts, I tracked him down. When I called him and told him I was from Chattanooga, he was reluctant to say much. He wanted to make sure I wasn't connected to the folks who might have played a role in his exit.

I assured him I wasn't a bad guy. I told him how much he influenced me, and what a big role he had played in my career. I confessed to pilfering a huge chunk of his act, and he graciously responded that he too, had borrowed from radio guys he had heard in his youth.

We had more conversations over the next few years, and we finally set up a time and place to meet. I was able to tell him face to face how important he was to me, and to others who had grown up listening to him, and I encouraged him to revisit Chattanooga after a 37-year absence. I learned he had led a normal life, building a successful career in and out of broadcasting.

"Chicky" with Luther Masingill in Chattanooga, 2010

"Bob," as I now call him, made a surprise visit to our annual reunion of local radio guys, and he got the royal treatment. He seemed genuinely touched that he was not only remembered, but deeply loved. Since then, he's been a frequent visitor, and he was able to reconnect with his former rival Luther Masingill, top-40 competitors Dale Anthony and Tommy Jett, and former co-workers Max Templeton and Garry Mac. Even better, other "kids" of my era have joined me in thanking him for having the courage to stir things up, and make us think.

It's been a real joy to establish a personal friendship with this once-mysterious figure who played such a huge role in my life and career. It's been even more joyful to watch him make so many friends in a town he once kept in the rear-view mirror. "Chicky-Poo" made a big impact in a short period of time, and his influence lives on today.

CHAPTER 6

Still Getting Schooled

It's the Principal of the Thing

For more than twenty years, I've been an education reporter. Most of the time, I've loved it. I go into more schools than the milk delivery guy. I regularly visit twenty different counties and school districts, and more than a hundred schools a year. I see the rich ones, the poor ones, the new ones, the crumbling ones.

How did this come to be? My boss called me in one day and said, "David, we think you should specialize in something. You need a regular beat." I replied, "That's fine, but just keep in mind that I like to be positive. Could you assign me something that doesn't have controversy, conflict, and politics?" He said, "Okay, how about schools?" I jumped at the chance. Now about that controversy, conflict, and politics: all I can say is, be careful what you wish for.

During this time, I've met hundreds of principals. Most of them understand my role. If their school has great test scores, or wins a big award, I should cover it. But if their school is vandalized, or a teacher gets in trouble, I should cover that too. Early on, a few principals hit me with this painful accusation: "You only put us on the news when it's something bad." Sadly, too often they were right. I pledged to visit them when something good was going on too, to give them positive coverage. That is still my goal.

As you might expect, being an education reporter, I get plenty of parental complaints. They used to arrive by letter, a few still come by phone, and now they're most often by e-mail or Facebook. Many of the complaints are about bus drivers and others are about teachers or principals. I look into each one. Most are the result of poor communication, and when the two sides actually talk, the problem resolves itself. However, some of them are valid complaints. If I do my job well, the problem either gets solved, or it becomes a story in which the public is informed about an issue that could affect them.

Certainly there are poor performing principals, just as there are poor performers in every occupation you can name, including news reporters. Still, I sympathize with principals, particularly those in public schools who feel like they're wearing huge targets on their backs.

The best principals are the ones who understand what I believe to be the three most important parts of their job. I often tell them they should spend 40% of their time on academics, 40% on discipline and 40% on public/parent relations. Yes, that adds up to 120%, but any principal will tell you they put in that extra time.

That is especially true for high school principals. The money is good, for sure. But who among us wants to unlock the door at 6 a.m., be responsible for the safety of 1,500 or more teenagers in this unpredictable world, and attend every athletic event, PTA meeting, dance and fundraiser? Folks, they earn their pay.

Most of them know they're the face of their school, and the good ones know how to set the right tone for their campus. One of my favorite principals is at a rural high school. Walking down the hall with him one day, I saw him spot a 9th grader out of dress code. "Boy, you better get that shirt tail in, or I'll whup your ass," he said in a stern tone of voice. He could tell I was a bit startled by his colorful choice of words. "Aw, that's nothing," he said. "I grew up with that boy's daddy. That's the only language he understands. And he knows I'm not really gonna whup his ass. I'd let his daddy handle that."

Such is the life of a high school principal. Middle school principals deal with raging hormones. Elementary principals get a lot of hugs, but have to wave off clingy parents. Above all, my experience has taught me this: I'd rather report on principals than be one.

What about MY School?

Students at Michigan Avenue Elementary School in Cleveland, TN, 2014

For those of us in the TV news business, winter is the busiest time of year. You know the drill: reporters on every mountain, endless video of salt spreaders and pothole patchers, and wise old news anchors reminding you to protect your water pipes. But by far the most cherished tradition is the school-closing list.

In our area, some say it all started with Luther Masingill, the late Chattanooga radio legend. I asked Luther how school closings were announced before he began his career in the early 1940s. He said, "I don't think schools ever closed back then. We just walked through the snow to get there." That answer was echoed by others, like the late principal Jack Benson. "We didn't close much," he said. "Most of the schools were in the neighborhoods. Some of us had to walk a mile or two, but if they had heat, they had school. If they didn't, you'd turn around and walk back home."

Another former principal, Bill Eldridge, said in the 1950s he would hold classes for whoever showed up. "If you couldn't make it, or the bus couldn't get to your house, we didn't count you absent back then," he said. "The schools got money from the state based on attendance, so we would lose money if they counted all the absences."

But eventually, schools started closing, and superintendents learned the quickest way to spread the news was to call Luther and other radio deejays. (There was little TV activity until the 1970s, as local morning newscasts were either brief or non-existent.) The busiest days of Luther's career included nonstop phone calls, with school officials trying to get through. At the same time, thousands of kids were calling to ask if their school was closed. Luther would compile an alphabetical list of counties, meaning the kids in Walker and Whitfield counties would have to sit tight as he waded through the Bradleys, the Dades, and the Jacksons.

When I got into radio, I quickly learned the rules: be nice to the callers, read the closings on-air frequently, and keep one ear on Luther because the school officials always called him first. It was also important to make sure no one was tricking us. Sometimes a bold 7th grader would call in, attempt to lower his voice, and say, "This is Mr. Elliott from Dade County. All schools is closed today." I'd say, "Uh, really, Mr. Elliott? I'm a little busy right now, could you give me your phone number so I can call you right back?" (Pause) "Click!" Busted. We had to be creative in the pre-caller ID days.

Later, TV got into the act. The two-hour morning newscasts allowed plenty of time to show a list of cancellations, including business closings. It also inspired a few other pranksters. One morning someone called our newsroom, asking us to add "Anthony's House of Cheese" to the list. A producer, flooded with legitimate calls, dutifully took down the information and entered it into the computerized list. For several hours, at the top of the business closing list, was "Anthony's House of Cheese," which of course, didn't exist. But all day, some guy was laughing, watching this go out on TV to thousands of people. We tightened up after that. Although frankly, as a cheese lover, I think someone should start a House of Cheese.

We also took live phone calls on the air. Much like Forrest Gump said about that box of chocolates, you never know what you're going to get. As a guest from the local electricity provider fielded calls about power outages, one woman was very upset. "Why," she wondered, "isn't my power back on? I'm looking out my window toward the road, and that car's got his lights on, so he's got power. Why don't I?"

No matter how clear the information may be these days, there are constant misunderstandings. We've learned that many people misread "Chattooga" County in northwest Georgia, assuming it is "Chattanooga" County in Tennessee, which does not exist. Unfortunately, not everyone is aware of that.

I have also learned that teachers are the best drivers in the world. They must be, because how many times have you heard this announcement? *"Due to hazardous driving conditions, there will be no school tomorrow. However, teachers and staff must report at the regular time."* Uh, wait. I thought you said driving conditions were hazardous? Oh well, I guess teachers know the secret passageways that have been de-iced.

So I've hatched a plan. One day, perhaps on my final day on the job, if it's really, really snowy, and truly every school is closed, I'd like to issue this statement:

"We are announcing with 100% certainty, that EVERY SINGLE SCHOOL in the universe will be closed today. This includes all schools in every city, every town, every county, public, private, boarding, religious, home, charter, technical, elementary, middle, high, colleges, junior colleges, universities, online, virtual, vocational, medical, dental, barber, beauty, business, GED, adult, preschool, pre-K, kindergarten, nursery, driving, Sunday

School, Vacation Bible, and even schools of fish. Every one of them, in every state, in every commonwealth, in every nation, on every continent, on every planet will be closed today. There are no exceptions. Enjoy your day off, everyone!"

Within a few seconds, I guarantee someone would ask, "But what about MY school?"

Making Eye Contact with the Graduating Class

Graduating seniors at Hamilton Heights High School in Chattanooga, 2013

I get to speak to high school seniors frequently, especially around graduation time. Some even ask me for a little advice. I always give it my best shot.

I figure that within a decade after they graduate, many of them will be doing a job that has yet to be invented. That's both exciting and a little scary. Think about these words: Twitter, Instagram, Pandora, Hulu, Google, iPhone, iPad, Snapchat, Pinterest. We hadn't heard those words a few years ago. Now our teens can't live without them. What will the new words be in the next decade?

I asked for guidance from my own sons, who are recent college graduates. I said, "Guys, you've been there. What would you tell them?" They said, "Show up for class, be on time, and get to know your instructors. Make sure they know your face and your name." As simple as it sounds, a lot of new college students don't show up for class often enough, and unlike high school, no one's trying to track you down when you're absent. But if you show up on time, and you develop a relationship with your instructors, it can pay off at exam time. They're more likely to give you help when you need it. Perhaps showing up really is half the battle.

I believe school is never really out. Long after you get your diploma, there will be joy about learning something new. As much as I love music, every day I hear a song and discover some words, an instrument, or a meaning I hadn't known before. Even when I figure out how to do something new on my phone, I have that same smile from when I learned the multiplication tables.

I would tell seniors that the high school teachers they have long feared, now have a new role: lifetime friends. I would tell them that money can indeed come in handy, but it sure doesn't bring you love or happiness. Watch the news and you'll see a lot of angry, sad millionaires, every day.

I would tell them how much I admire people who win without bragging, and who lose without making excuses. The way I see it, if you're good at something, even if you're the best, you will never have to tell everyone. They will know it.

I would tell them that this old saying is true: "If you find a job you love, you'll never work a day in your life." Thankfully, that happened to me.

I would offer some brief driving tips: buckle up, use your headlights in the rain and fog, and never text while driving. I don't like to read names on the news unless it's for something good.

I would say that even in this age of texting and tweeting, personal contact is still the best way to communicate. Set aside some time every day to put your device away. Look at people, right in their eyes. Talk to them, listen to them. At any college campus, you'll see students, with heads down, randomly bumping into each other, and carelessly walking into traffic. This is not a good trend.

I would tell them many employers still value good spelling and punctuation. All those cute abbreviations and shortcuts used on social media may not go over so well in the job application process.

I would tell them to be careful with their social media posts. Potential employers will check them out, and somehow they last forever.

Once you get a job, if a customer (or boss) tries to get your attention, and you can't hear them over your earbuds, you may soon be looking for another job.

I would tell them when their doctor says to wear plenty of sunscreen, he's not kidding! I hope today's teens do a better job of following those instructions than I did.

And I would tell them to try to do something nice for someone every day, without being asked. That always seems to put the cherry on my hot fudge cake.

I've Seen Teachers

*East Side Elementary (Chattanooga) teacher Mandy Love
taking her students on a field trip in 2015*

Many of my school news stories cover the leaky roofs, the fights, the weapons, the dress code complaints, and the overcrowded classrooms and buses.

The majority of school stories, however, involve positive aspects of education. Many of those stories go relatively unnoticed.

I suppose that's human nature. Some weeks, nine out of ten school-related stories will be positive. I often get no feedback about those stories, but the negative one is sure to strike a chord. It will be waved in my face repeatedly as an example of negative media. This occurs, despite the fact some of these stories help spur elected officials into noticing the problems and spending the money to solve them.

Through it all, I've tried to become a keen observer. I've seen some amazing people in those school hallways, and I'd like to tell you about them.

I've seen:

Teachers who arrive early and stay late.

Principals who constantly brag on their faculty and staff, and will tell you they have the best anywhere.

Spouses, parents and children of teachers and principals, who paint, sweep, and do whatever it takes to make the classroom an inviting place for children. None of them get a dime from taxpayers for their work.

Teachers who take it upon themselves to set a good example by looking their students in the eye, speaking clearly, giving a firm handshake, dressing professionally, and writing thank-you notes for kindnesses shown.

Teachers who attend and cheer at their students' athletic events, whether they understand or even like the sport. It's their team, and they are in the stands to show their support.

Teachers who spend much of their personal time acting as surrogate parents, nurses or psychologists.

Art, music, and drama teachers who take children from the poorest homes, and find the hidden talent that allows them to shine as artists, singers, dancers, or actors.

Vocational/technical teachers who turn students into well-paid welders, mechanics, carpenters, beauticians, graphic artists, or computer programmers.

Teachers of gifted and advanced students who find ways to challenge them and make them aspire to be even better.

Teachers of the physically disabled. They are the angels among us who perform miracles every day. From the tiniest preschoolers to the brawniest teens, these superhuman teachers tend to their every need. They nurture, feed, and lift up those children in every way.

Coaches, club and cheerleader sponsors, band directors, and music teachers who are forced to spend much of their spare time being fund raisers.

Teachers who spend a full workday dealing with homework and testing, who then go home and spend an entire evening helping their own children with these same chores.

Teachers who see that their students get something for their birthday, or for Christmas, because in some homes, this will not be done.

Teachers who request to be transferred to a low-performing, low income school, because they know those students need something extra.

Teachers who are greeted warmly in public by someone who says, "Mrs. Smith, do you remember me from fifth grade?" More often than not, she remembers. That always amazes me, because Mrs. Smith has taught hundreds of fifth-graders. But to each of them, she's the only fifth-grade teacher they ever had.

Teachers who spend time in the summer decorating their classroom with maps and posters, only to learn they will have to take it all down and start over when they're transferred to another room, or even another school.

Teachers and principals who perform all sorts of stunts as incentives to get students fired up about meeting their goals. From being duct-taped to the wall, to taking pies in the face, they do whatever it takes.

Teachers who buy clothing and shoes for their students, take them trick-or-treating, or make sure they have Thanksgiving dinner.

High school counselors, who make sure students are ready to take college entrance exams, fill out job applications, and perform well in job interviews.

Teachers who come to work even when they're ill because they know a qualified substitute won't be available, and they don't want to burden a fellow teacher, or shortchange their students.

Teachers and principals who keep working long past their retirement eligibility date, because they love what they do.

Coaches who go out of their way to pick up a child and take him to practice, knowing that sports may be what keeps him in school.

Every day, I see something new. I hope this helps explains why I admire so many of the people I've met on the school beat.

Many of us don't take time to say it, but believe me, teachers and principals, you are appreciated. Congratulations on being a part of this most challenging and honorable profession. You get to teach!

Back-to-School Funnies!

First, a classic teacher joke. The kindergarten children brought presents for their teacher, Mrs. Jones.

Brandon handed Mrs. Jones a gift. The teacher knew Brandon's father was a florist. She held up the box and said, "Oh, you got me some flowers!"

"That's right!" shouted Brandon.

Then Nicole handed Mrs. Jones a gift. The teacher knew Nicole's mother owned a candy store. She held up the box and said, "Oh, I just know this is a box of chocolates!"

"That's right!" squealed Nicole.

The next gift was from Andy. The teacher knew Andy's father owned a liquor store. Mrs. Jones held up the box and saw a wet spot. It was leaking, just a little. She touched a drop with her finger and tasted it.

"Mmmm, is it fine wine?" she asked.

"No ma'am," Andy answered. Mrs. Jones touched another drop to her tongue.

"Well then it must be champagne, right Andy?" she asked.

"No ma'am," Andy replied.

"Well then, I give up. What is it?" she said.

He grinned from ear to ear and said, "It's a puppy!"

That brings us to my favorite Facebook posts, from actual parents and students. You can't make this stuff up:

First, "You said schools should teach cursive writing. I say no! My children have already learned too many cursive words from those movies we get at RedBox."

Then, there's this one: "You keep saying bullies pray on small-er children. I didn't think they allowed that in school."

From a student: "Who cares about this stupid dress code any-way? Next year I'll be in collage."

Another student wrote, "I don't like the rules we have here. We need a new principle."

A snow day post: "Why are they making us go to school tomoro? It don't make any since."

Another snow day post: "The news said schools was closed in clement weather. What does that even mean?"

One parent weighed in the day after the snow had melted: "You say Hamilton County schools will be on regular schedule Monday. But what is the time they will be open?"

Another parent asked, "Why do the schools keep buying computers? I think it is a waist of tax money."

Demonstrating the "smart look" with students at
East Ridge (TN) Elementary School, 2015

I love to visit elementary schools. If you want a huge dose of honesty, just talk to first and second graders.

I visited a second-grade class, and as I started talking to the kids, I thought I'd try to make them laugh. So I looked around the room, inhaled the air, waved my arms and said, "What a great classroom! It smells like EDUCATION in here!" I barely got it out of my mouth when a little boy raised his hand and said, "No sir, that's Lysol. Miss Kathy wiped down everything before you came in."

When I visited the second graders at my old school in Alabama, it was a real treat. I told them that I, too, was once in second grade. One girl looked at me with those wide eyes and exclaimed, "I can only imagine what your village was like."

I got more specific with them, and told them I had been a second grader in their classroom, surrounded by those very same walls. A little boy, quite seriously raised his hand, pointed at his young, twenty-something teacher, and asked, "Was Miss Smith your teacher?" She may have kept him after school that day, I'm not sure.

I also visited an elementary school on a day when Miss Tennessee paid a visit, in full beauty-queen mode. The tiara, the sash, big hair, lots of makeup and a tight outfit revealing a shapely figure. After spending the better part of an hour talking about the evils of drugs and the importance of staying in school, she invited questions. The kids were shy at first, so she said, "Go ahead, you can ask me about whatever is on your mind." A third-grade boy jumped up, raised his hand, and shouted, "Are you a Kardashian?"

I was about to read *Clifford the Big Red Dog* to a second-grade class, and I did my usual pep talk about reading. When I asked if they loved to read, they all raised their hand. I asked if second grade was fun, and again, all hands went up. When I asked, "Are you looking forward to third grade?" only a few hands went up.

"So are you worried about third grade?" I asked. Immediately, they began voicing their concerns about more homework, and learning the times tables.

I started in with the sales pitch. "You're going to LOVE third grade!" I said. "You're going to read a lot more, and you'll get even smarter than you are now!" I was on a roll. "Then soon you'll be in middle school, and you'll get REALLY smart!" I couldn't leave well enough alone. "And then you'll be in high school, and that's going to be even MORE fun!" A seven-year-old girl put up her hand as if to stop me, and said, "Dude, slow down! We're only little!"

CHAPTER 7

From My Record Collection

Fun Facts: The Songs You Grew Up With

There's usually a song in my head, which causes me to ask my wife, "What song are you thinking about now?" Ever the hip chick, her answer is always something by Fleet Foxes or a little-known Van Morrison track. I'm more likely to have a burned-out oldie spinning around in my noggin. Even worse, if I try to be clever and change the lyrics, CCR's "Who'll Stop the Rain" becomes "Who'll Stop Lorraine," and Huey Lewis's "If This Is It," turns into "Is This a Zit?"

When I hear "Angel of the Morning," Merilee Rush sings, "Just touch my cheek before you leave me," but I change it to "Just brush my teeth . . ." Maybe it's an old disc jockey thing. Our hearing is so shot, it's a wonder we can hear anything at all.

Gordon Lightfoot's "Wreck of the Edmund Fitzgerald" certainly wasn't written this way, but when he opens the song by singing, "The legend lives on from the Chippewa on down, of the big lake they called Gitche Gumee," I always sing "peg leg" instead of "big lake." That's always what it sounded like to me. Sorry, Gordon.

No matter how hard they try, that Sandpipers song, "Guantanamera" will always be "One Ton Tomato" to me. "I want a one-ton tomato . . ."

I've read that Hugo Montenegro's classic theme to "The Good, The Bad, and The Ugly," includes chants and grunts that aren't really words at all. But they are to me. I sing something different every time I hear it. It may be "shrimp boat." Or it could be "French toast." Others have suggested "Ringgold" or "Red Bull." Who really knows?

In the 1960s, Dion had a hit with "Runaround Sue." The doo-wop background singers, according to the lyric sheet, are singing, "Hey, hey, um de hey, de hey, de hey, hey, um de hey, de hey, de hey." I don't think so. When I was a kid, the great Chattanooga DJ Chickamauga Charlie sang along with it one morning, totally convincing me that what they were REALLY saying was, "Hurt, hurt . . . bumped my head, and it hurt, hurt. Bumped my head and it hurt, hurt.." Ever since then, that's how I sing along with "Runaround Sue." My apologies to you too, Dion.

By the way, you can't always trust the labels on those records you bought when you were a kid. Did you think "Wasted on the Way" was by Crosby, Stills and Nash? Nope. Truth is, it was sung by only Stephen Stills and Graham Nash. This may come as a shock, but David Crosby was so "wasted" that day, he didn't show up for the recording session.

Remember "Fooled Around and Fell In Love" by Elvin Bishop? That was the name of the artist on the label. I played that hundreds of times, telling you it was Elvin Bishop singing that tune. Well, it was his band, and Elvin did write the song. But the man who sang it was Mickey Thomas, who was later the lead singer on "We Built This City" by Starship. Great, now that one's in my head.

How many times have you heard "Someday We'll Be To-gether," and the DJ told you it was the final song recorded by Diana Ross and the Supremes, before Diana left the group to become a solo act? Actually, Diana had already split. She wanted it to be her first solo record, but Motown thought it would sell better as a Supremes farewell. The background singers were actually Julia and Maxine Waters, who were never Supremes. But, Motown was right: it became a number-one hit.

I used to get requests for "I Saw the Light" by Carole King, but it was actually sung by Todd Rundgren. That could be because Todd said he was inspired by another Carole King hit, "Sweet Seasons."

Many listeners were sure that "(I Love You) More Today Than Yesterday" (sung by the late Pat Upton of Spiral Starecase) was done by Stevie Wonder. No doubt Stevie would have nailed it, but it wasn't him.

In fact, one of Stevie's biggest hits was actually a group effort that included people whose names you've probably never heard. The opening verse of "You Are the Sunshine of My Life" is sung first by Jim Gilstrap, and then Lani Groves. Stevie doesn't start singing until later. If you're like me, you probably thought he was just changing his voice.

Who else thought Glen Campbell's "Wichita Lineman" was about the largest city in Kansas? Me too, but no. Songwriter Jim Webb actually had Washita County, Oklahoma in mind. Glen said he changed it to "Wichita" during the recording session because it sounded better.

It may also surprise you to learn that some songs we thought were about boy-girl break-ups, were about something else entirely. In that great 1975 hit "How Long (Has This Been Going On)" by Ace, lead singer Paul Carrack makes you think it's about a girl who was cheating on him. Truth is, the song was written in response to a band member who was leaving the group.

David Gates of the '70s group Bread had me thinking he'd give "Everything I Own" just to have a certain girl back again. He later revealed it wasn't about a former girlfriend. His father had died young, and he was the subject of David's emotional lament. Now these words really hit home, don't they? "Is there someone you know, you're loving them so, but taking them all for granted . . . You may lose them one day, someone takes them away, and they don't hear the words you long to say . . ."

That's the power of music. So often, a gifted songwriter is able to speak for us, better than we can say it ourselves. That is, as long as we can understand the words.

The Worst Songs Ever!

"It makes my ears bleed!" "It makes me feel sick!" "It makes my hair stand on end!"

These are some of the comments I received in my quest to identify the Worst Songs Ever. I polled readers online and in newspapers, and there was no shortage of nominations.

Although the 1970s is considered to be The Bad Songs Decade (it gave us "Run Joey Run," "Convoy," and "Kung Fu Fighting"), there were plenty of duds recorded before the 70s, and there are more on the radio today.

Meghan Trainor's 2014 ode to big backsides, "It's All About That Bass" got its share of votes ("I'm skinny and I can't help it, leave me alone") along with Taylor Swift's "Shake It Off" ("We TURN it off, every time it comes on") and the *Frozen* anthem, "Let It Go." ("Please tell your ten-year-old daughter to like another song!")

Also from recent years, "What Does the Fox Say?" caught plenty of scorn ("I know what I'd tell the fox"), along with the Black Eyed Peas "My Humps" ("It belongs in the Bad Song Hall of Fame"), and "Who Let the Dogs Out" by the Baha Men ("They should have unleashed those dogs in the studio!")

1990s music lovers had plenty to say, from Hanson's "MmmBop" ("Mmmm, no!") to the bubblegum-flavored "Barbie Girl" ("I'll bet even Ken hates that one") and Ricky Martin's "Living La Vida Loca" ("I know all the words, and I'm not proud of that.")

Whitney Houston's 1992 recording of Dolly Parton's "I Will Always Love You" also came under fire. ("Pure howling. It brings shivers from head to toe!")

The 1980s are remembered for MTV and big-hair, but some haven't forgiven that decade for Starship's "We Built This City," ("From the band that gave us some of the best songs of the '60s? Did they sober up or something?"), Toni Basil's cheerleader anthem "Mickey," ("I pulled a muscle trying to switch to another station"), and every song recorded by Rick Astley ("Never Gonna Give You Up"), Boy George ("Karma Chameleon"), and the B-52's ("Rock Lobster").

Stevie Nicks has plenty of fans, but some of her 1980s-era lyrics were singled out for special attention. Her 1981 hit "Edge of Seventeen" includes this line: "Just like the white winged dove, sings a song sounds like she's singing, ooh, baby, ooh, baby, ooh." ("I'm sorry, I don't get it. Does anyone?")

The 1970s decade is in a league of its own. There were nominations for the Temptations epic "Papa Was a Rolling Stone," ("Is it over yet? Please, make it stop"), Terry Jacks' tear-jerker "Seasons in The Sun" ("We had joy, we had fun, until this sappy song came on"), and 3 Dog Night's ever-present "Joy To The World" ("If I hear Jeremiah was a bullfrog one more time, my head will explode!")

Paul McCartney's 1970s output incurred the wrath of many, starting with "Silly Love Songs."("After writing all those Beatles classics, he must have run out of ideas.") The lyrics of McCartney's "Let 'em In" were quoted: "Someone's knockin' at the door, somebody's ringing the bell, do me a favor, open the door, let 'em in." ("Did he make a bet that his fans would buy anything? I guess he won.")

Then there was America's "Horse with No Name," ("At first I thought it was Neil Young, but he wouldn't stoop that low"), Lobo's "Me and You and a Dog Named Boo" ("Boo is the right word"), and Debby Boone's "You Light Up My Life." ("A one-hit wonder. No wonder.")

That decade must also be held accountable for "Billy Don't Be a Hero," "The Night The Lights Went Out in Georgia," "The Night Chicago Died," "Delta Dawn," and the infamous "Muskrat Love." Who can forget these words: "Muskrat Susie, Muskrat Sam, do the jitterbug out in muskrat land, and they shimmy, and Sam is so skinny." Yes, I played that on the radio. Please forgive me.

The '60s gave us the never-ending "MacArthur Park" by Richard Harris ("Somebody, get that cake out of the rain already; it's been 50 years!") There were also votes for "The Lion Sleeps Tonight" and "Sugar Sugar." (True confession: those are two of my guilty pleasures).

Even though we only hear them over the holidays, several Christmas songs were named: Jose Feliciano's earworm "Feliz Navidad," the too-sexy-for-some "Santa Baby," McCartney's repetitive "Wonderful Christmas Time" and the unfortunately unforgettable "Grandma Got Run Over by a Reindeer." ("Whoever got rich from that should send us all a rebate!")

That brings us to the three Worst Songs Ever, at least according to my respondents. Number three is "Mambo # 5" by Lou Bega from 1999 ("I've seen too many drunks try to dance to this at wedding receptions"), and number two is the 1995 dance sensation "Macarena." ("Every time they sing the word Macarena, it's followed by the sound my cat makes when he spits up a hairball.")

So what's the Worst Song Ever? It's another '70s stinker, Rick Dees's "Disco Duck," which topped the charts in 1976. Can't argue with this one, folks. Some of us truly have a good ear for bad music.

Why Isn't There a Movie about Charley Pride?

Country Music Hall of Fame member Charley Pride

Hollywood loves to make movies about music icons. Often, but not always, they're biographies of dead performers. Think Jim Morrison, Elvis Presley, and James Brown. In Ray Charles' case, the movie *Ray* was completed just before he died. I saw *Love and Mercy*, which depicts the life of Beach Boy Brian Wilson (still among the living), and while it's hard to watch on many levels, it does feature his amazing musical skills.

I'm surprised no one has made a movie about Stevie Wonder's life, because it could be a good one. His father made a living by selling his mother's body on the streets. Blind since birth, he was raised just like his siblings. He was sent out to play, and if he fell into a ditch, that was considered a life lesson. As a teen, he was on the road with the Temptations (in every sense of the word). He then wrote and performed more hit songs than anyone during a 20-year period while bedding numerous women and fathering several children. Let's just say it's a life made for the big screen.

Then there's Charley Pride, whose story is equally incredible. You don't hear Charley's name much these days. He hasn't had a radio hit in more than a quarter-century. Most of his best-sellers date back to the early 80s: even some of the classic country stations don't go back that far. In fact, I'd say most filmmakers would give a thumbs-down to a screenplay about an artist whose fans are a few decades north of the "Captain America" audience.

That's a shame. Hollywood celebrated the life of baseball pioneer Jackie Robinson in *42*. Queen Latifah starred as Bessie Smith in a popular HBO movie. So why hasn't Charley Pride's life story been told? It's been rumored for years, but has never made it to the screen. I'd love to see it happen in the man's lifetime.

Here's the short version. He was born in Mississippi, to a family of poor sharecroppers. He was one of eleven children. He learned to play guitar as a child, and also excelled in baseball. He pitched in the Negro American league starting at the age of 14. A year later, he signed with the New York Yankees, playing in their minor league system.

At 15, he was traded (with another player) to a competing team for a bus. Yes, a bus. He served two years in the Army, then returned to baseball, playing in the Cincinnati Reds organization. At the age of 20, he got serious about music. Country music. Let's pause here for a moment. He's black, and trying to make it in country music in 1958 America. There's a pretty good movie here so far, don't you think?

Yet this is where it truly gets interesting. After struggling for a few years, he was signed to RCA Records by legendary producer-guitarist Chet Atkins. Atkins knew a star when he heard one. He had discovered most of RCA's biggest sellers of that era, including Jim Reeves and Skeeter Davis. But with Charley Pride, RCA was dealing with, shall we say, a unique situation. So the label put out his records, with no pictures of the singer.

He was billed as "Country Charley Pride." For the first two years, radio deejays and listeners had no idea what he looked like. His song "Just Between You and Me" came out in 1966, and hit the top 10.

That song was the first in a string of sixty top-ten country hits, including "Kiss an Angel Good Morning," which also went top-20 on the pop charts.

He was the first black member of the Grand Ole Opry, a 2000 inductee into the Country Music Hall of Fame, was honored with a star on the Hollywood Walk of Fame, has performed at the Super Bowl, the World Series, the Baseball Hall of Fame, and at concert venues worldwide.

Earl Freudenberg, who played the hits at Chattanooga's WDOD in the 1960s, remembers when Charley "came out" to country audiences, including a sold-out crowd at Memorial Auditorium. "He'd appear on stage, sing one of his hits, and say, I don't look like I sound, do I? Up until then, RCA asked us not to say anything about him being black. They'd say, just play his records, so that's what we did."

I think Charley Pride's story is one of the most amazing in show business history. Although it's still unusual today for a black artist to make it big in the country music field (Darius Rucker is a recent exception), in the 1960s, it was seemingly impossible. Charley has some great stories to tell, many of which are in his 1994 autobiography. About his first concert appearance, much dreaded by RCA executives: "Once I opened my mouth and started singing, they liked what they heard."

It's way past time his life was celebrated on the big screen. What an inspiration he has been to us all. Come on Hollywood, let's do this!

Greatest Country Songs Ever?
Rolling Stone Missed a Few

There's one surefire way to get attention if you're publishing a magazine. Just make a list of the best songs, TV shows, cars, or any category that will trigger a debate. Leave off somebody's favorite, and they'll let you know. In 2014 *Rolling Stone*, not exactly my go-to source for country music information, stirred the pot by naming "The 25 Greatest Country Songs of All Time."

I knew that I would disagree with some of their selections, but I read it anyway. To be fair, there isn't a bad song on the list:

1. "I Walk the Line" – Johnny Cash (1956)
2. "Crazy" – Patsy Cline (1961)
3. "I'm So Lonesome I Could Cry" – Hank Williams (1949)
4. "He Stopped Loving Her Today" – George Jones (1980)
5. "Standing on the Corner (Blue Yodel No. 9")" – Jimmie Rodgers (1930)
6. "Stand By Your Man" – Tammy Wynette (1968)
7. "You Don't Know Me" – Ray Charles (1962)
8. "Mama Tried" – Merle Haggard (1968)
9. "Jolene" – Dolly Parton (1973)
10. "Mammas, Don't Let Your Babies Grow Up to Be Cowboys" – Waylon Jennings and Willie Nelson (1978)
11. "Man of Constant Sorrow" – Stanley Brothers (1951)
12. "I've Got a Tiger by the Tail" – Buck Owens and the Buckaroos (1964)

13. "Blue Moon of Kentucky" – Bill Monroe and the Blue Grass Boys (1947)
14. "Settin' the Woods on Fire" – Hank Williams (1952)
15. "It Wasn't God Who Made Honky Tonk Angels" – Kitty Wells (1952)
16. "Wichita Lineman" – Glen Campbell (1968)
17. "New San Antonio Rose" – Bob Wills & His Texas Playboys (1940)
18. "All My Ex's Live in Texas" – George Strait (1987)
19. "Don't Come Home a Drinkin' (With Lovin' On Your Mind)" – Loretta Lynn (1966)
20. "The Gambler" – Kenny Rogers (1978)
21. "Can the Circle Be Unbroken" – Carter Family (1935)
22. "Walking the Floor Over You" – Ernest Tubb (1941)
23. "If You've Got the Money, I've Got the Time" – Lefty Frizzell (1950)
24. "Mean" - Taylor Swift (2010)
25. "Take This Job and Shove It" – Johnny Paycheck (1977)

Yes, this is a great list of songs, but it is wide open for nit-picking. If you're going to boldly select the 25 greatest country songs ever, how do you leave out "Hello Darlin'" by Conway Twitty? Nothing says "country" like Conway.

Conway not only failed to make the top 25, *Rolling Stone* didn't include any of his songs in its expanded top 100 list either! And he's not the only one. Believe it or not, neither did the Statler Brothers. I could have chosen any number of Statler songs, but the *Rolling Stone* writers did not. They certainly deserve to be on this list.

If you look at the years of the songs the magazine selected, you might notice a huge gap. There's nothing between 1987 (George Strait's "All My Ex's") and 2010 (Taylor Swift's

"Mean"). So in their opinion, Taylor Swift is the only artist who achieved greatness in country music during that 23-year period. Someone needs to introduce them to Alan Jackson, who also failed to crack their top 100.

1992's "Chattahoochee" was one in a long string of hits for Jackson, who has dominated the past quarter-century along with Garth Brooks, Clint Black, Randy Travis, Brad Paisley, Vince Gill, Shania Twain, Don Williams, Alabama, Emmylou Harris, Brooks & Dunn, Keith Whitley and many others who got little or no mention on the *Rolling Stone* Top 100, much less the top 25. Yet somehow, they included "Goodbye Earl" by the Dixie Chicks, "Convoy" by C. W. McCall, "Redneck Woman" by Gretchen Wilson and "The Happiest Girl in the Whole USA" by Donna Fargo.

Yes, they were all big hits, but should they be among the 100 Greatest of All Time, while totally leaving out Hank Williams Jr.? "Family Tradition" was released in 1979, a few years after two near-death experiences: a suicide attempt and a mountain-climbing accident. If anyone has led a country music life, it's Hank, but he gets little respect from *Rolling Stone*, or the music industry, which has inexplicably kept him out of the Country Music Hall of Fame.

Here's another head-scratcher: one of the greatest country songwriters of the 20th century was totally snubbed by *Rolling Stone*: Kris Kristofferson. Any or all of the following songs could have been included: "Why Me, Lord?" "For the Good Times." "Me and Bobby McGee." "Sunday Morning Coming Down." My personal favorite is "Help Me Make It Through the Night," a Kristofferson classic first recorded by Sammi Smith.

She had me at "Take the ribbon from my hair . . ." This is one of those rare recordings in which every single element is spot-on perfect. The strings, the voice, the lyrics, the mood. Kristofferson originally wrote it from a male point of view, but Smith effortlessly turned it around. "It's so sad to be alone . . ." You can hear the yearning, the despair. How this incredible song missed the cut at *Rolling Stone* is a mystery to me.

So, obviously, *Rolling Stone* has about as much business picking the best country songs ever as, well, I do. I have absolutely zero experience in the country music business.

Pointing to a billboard touting my country music radio show,
which never actually aired

Although there was this one time. In 1984, I had been on TV for about a year, and was convinced that my leaving radio had been a huge mistake. Chattanooga country station WDOD had a new general manager who wanted to change the station's morning show. He recruited me to do battle with the new US-101, which had emerged as a strong competitor. I said yes, and he proceeded to put up thirty full-color *Carroll Country* billboards all over town. I was fired up and ready to begin my country music career. I turned in my notice to the TV station, and started sizing up boots and cowboy hats. Then suddenly, the guy who had hired me, got fired by the station owner. (Maybe he spent too much money on billboards?) I got cold feet, realizing my imminent career move may not have been such a great idea.

I told my sob story to my TV employers, who kindly let me stay. So, I never got to play a country song on the radio. But I've heard a few of them, which makes me as qualified as *Rolling Stone* to comment on the best songs ever. Besides, "Swingin" by John Anderson isn't on their list. I rest my case.

There's a Bathroom on the Right

It should be obvious by now: I love rock 'n roll oldies. I don't even pretend to be a music snob. You can have your trendy new music, your deep album cuts and even your high-falutin' classical music. Give me those hook-laden top-40 pop songs that I can sing along with.

There's almost always some song from the '60s, '70s or '80s blaring from my car speakers, and that's me with the windows up, sparing you the pain. When Van Morrison's song "Wild Night" comes on the radio, I try to sing along. I have no idea what Van is saying, and I defy you to figure it out as well. No fair going to Google and reading the lyrics. I can't do that while I'm driving, and neither should you.

Van just wails along, mumbling and slurring. That makes it different from many songs I misunderstood on my cheap AM radio speaker. For instance, if you thought CCR's John Fogerty was singing "There's a bathroom on the right," (a bad moon on the rise) I was right there with you. In fact, Fogerty has heard the joke so often, he sometimes sings it that way on stage.

Speaking of CCR and Fogerty, remember "Lookin' Out My Back Door?" The one about tambourines and elephants, all playing in the band? In the first verse, Fogerty sings, "Look at all the happy creatures dancing on the lawn." When I was a kid, I thought he was saying "happy preachers dancing on the lawn." Now there's a visual image for you.

Same goes for another big CCR hit, "Have You Ever Seen the Rain?" Some folks swore he was looking for a lady named Lorraine. "I wanna know . . . have you ever seen . . . Lorraine."

Lorraine made a comeback in someone else's song. Remember Johnny Nash's hit, "I Can See Clearly Now, Lorraine has gone." Lorraine sure got around, didn't she?

She wasn't the only one. How about Leslie? Remember "Groovin' (on a Sunday afternoon)" by the Rascals? Near the end of the song, the lead singer says, "Life would be ecstasy, you and me endlessly, groovin." But many of us thought he said "you and me *and Leslie*." I spent years wondering who Leslie was.

One of my most-requested songs at KZ-106 back in the 80s was Foreigner's "Jukebox Hero." I do remember one kid who called in a request for "Juice Box Hero." I think he was serious. I also got requests for a song believed to be "Chug-a-Lug," which upon further investigation turned out to be "Jungle Love" by Steve Miller.

My all-time favorite Elvis Presley song is "Suspicious Minds." Imagine my surprise when a friend began singing along to the dramatic opening line, "We're caught in a trap." He thought the King was about to send his unfaithful partner home in a taxi: "We're calling a cab."

My former radio DJ friends on Facebook remember some others. Steve Hill from Dalton, Georgia recalled some 1970s-era requests for "Willard Go Round In Circles." The song they wanted to hear was Billy Preston's "Will It Go Round In Circles," but now I'll think of Willard Scott getting dizzy, every time I hear it.

Roger Davis told of a friend who went to the record store and asked for a copy of "My God the Spark." As in, "My God the spark, is melting in the dark . . ." Now I have a reason to listen to "MacArthur Park."

Stu Wright remembers when Johnny Rivers's 1966 hit "Secret Agent Man" was misheard by many as "Secret Asian Man." Frankly, that's what it sounds like Johnny is saying.

Also in the '60s, the McCoys had a big hit that still gets played at wedding parties today: "Hang On Sloopy." But on the static-filled AM radios of that era, many folks thought they were singing, "Hang on Stupid . . . Stupid, hang on!" (Thanks to Mike Miranda for that one.)

Many of us fondly remember a soul hit from 1971, Jean Knight's "Mr. Big Stuff" ("who do you think you are"). Bryan McIntyre remembers getting requests for "Mr. Pit Stop." Maybe they were NASCAR fans? And now that I hear it again, they weren't too far off.

Jimmy Rowe recalls Elton John's version of "Lucy in the Sky with Diamonds," with that memorable line about "the girl with kaleidoscope eyes." He said someone called and wanted to hear the one where "the girl with colitis walks by." There aren't many songs about people with colon problems, but at least one person thought this one was.

My wife Cindy was in her twenties before she figured out that in "My Cherie Amour," Stevie Wonder wants to "share your little distant cloud," and not "your little sister Sal." My son Vince's faulty interpretation of lyrics dates back to his childhood. He heard Honey Cone sing "Gonna put it in the Want Ads," but to him it sounded like "My brother has a wood ass." (His brother was puzzled by that one). Another family member was heard loudly singing along to the Hues Corporation's big hit "Rock the Boat." The very first line is "I'd like to know where . . . you got the notion." You can imagine how embarrassed she was, belting out, "I'd like to know where . . . you got *pollution*."

Quite often, the singers themselves are to blame. They're either intentionally garbling the lyrics ("Louie Louie" by the

Kingsmen), drowned out by the music (Mick Jagger, in "Tumbling Dice") or maybe they want to keep us guessing (Michael McDonald in most of his Doobie Brothers hits, like "What a Fool Believes").

Still, Tom Jones is loud and clear in the opening lines of "She's A Lady," when he belts out, "She's got style, she's got grace, she's a *wiener.*" I think you mean "winner," Sir Tom.

The Four Tops had millions of us dancing to "I Can't Help Myself," with its memorable refrain of "Sugar Pie, Honey Bunch." That didn't keep many of us from hearing "Sugar Fried Honey Butts."

When I hear Duran Duran's "Hungry Like a Wolf," I think my misheard version makes more sense than the real thing. To me it sounds like "I smell like a *sow,* I'm lost in a crowd." Actually, they're singing, "I smell like I sound." I'm sticking with the sow.

Some of us like to repeat the wrong words, even though the correct ones are loud and clear. Who among us hasn't enhanced Elton John's "Tiny Dancer," by singing out, "Hold me closer, *Tony Danza.*" Mr. Danza himself gets a kick out of that one. Or at least he did the first 500 times people sang it to him. It may be getting old to him by now, but it's still funny to me.

This even goes outside the border of music. In fourth grade, I had a pretty good handle on the Pledge of Allegiance, but an unnamed classmate (who may be reading this story, and is bigger than me) would routinely recite, "I pledge allegiance to the flag of the United States of America, and to the republic for *Richard Stands . . .*" He was surely among many who wondered, who is this Richard guy, and why is he always standing?

CHAPTER 8

A Little Local History

Why Do They Call It *The Ol' Johnny Bridge?*

During my career, I've welcomed many new reporters into Chattanooga. Since they're usually from out of town, they ask me a lot of questions. Like, "What's a Soddy Daisy?" And, "Is Georgia still trying to get your water?" Of course, there's always, "What's that smell?" if we're on the South Side near the chicken plant.

They ask me these questions because I've lived in the area all my life. I used to joke that you know you're getting old when you drive around saying, "See that parking lot? There used to be a Shakey's Pizza Parlor there." Or, "See that supermarket? That's where I went to school, before they tore it down." Yes, I've become that guy.

Olgiati Bridge, downtown Chattanooga, 2015

The most frequently asked question is about that six-lane span over the Tennessee River downtown. Sometimes it's "Why did they name it *The Ol' Johnny Bridge*? Who's Johnny?" Or, "Why did they name it *The Ol' Jolly Bridge*?" That is usually followed by, "I've never seen a jolly bridge; that doesn't make any sense." I've even heard traffic reporters mispronounce the name of our beloved bridge. Officially it's the Olgiati Bridge, named for Peter Rudolf "Rudy" Olgiati. Pronounced "OL-Jotty" with a long "O." So who is this bridge guy?

Longtime residents know he was Mayor Olgiati. With a name like that, you'd think he moved here from Pennsylvania or New Jersey, but no. He was born in Grundy County, in Gruetli, Tennessee in 1901. His mother was from Switzerland, his father was from Spain. His father died when he was six, and in 1913 his mother moved Rudy and his two younger brothers to the Alton Park area of Chattanooga. Young Rudy learned the building trade, moving up from bricklayer to superintendent of a large construction company. By the time he was in his thirties, he ran the city's busiest recreation center, Warner Park. In 1946, he was politically connected enough to be appointed to the City Commission, to fill out an unexpired term. He ran for, and won a full term in 1947, and then took on the incumbent mayor in 1951. He won that race too, and began a three-term, twelve-year run as Chattanooga's "boss." That term isn't used loosely.

J. B. Collins, who covered city politics for the *Chattanooga News-Free Press* for almost sixty years calls Olgiati "the last of a breed, the last of Chattanooga's political kings." Remembering a time when an elected official could control numerous voting precincts, Collins said, "He had power, and he knew how to use it to get his way. He really ran all the city departments. Nobody has that kind of power today." For most of his first two terms,

Olgiati used that power to get the attention of state and federal officials. He went after, and got $100 million in federal grants to build much of the infrastructure that would transform the city. He pushed for an expansion of Chattanooga's airport, calling the finished product "one of the best in the south." The 1950s ushered in interstate highway construction across the nation, and Olgiati felt Chattanooga's close proximity to big cities in each direction should make his city a priority. Chattanooga became the first of Tennessee's major cities to have a completed interstate system. Then came the bridge.

The bridge did not come without controversy. The Cedar Street Bridge, as it was known at first, was sorely needed. Since 1949, there was talk of a third downtown span to relieve congestion on the overcrowded Market and Walnut Street bridges. Engineers determined that new road construction could be accomplished in part by cutting off the top half of Cameron Hill, at one time a prominent downtown neighborhood. It had fallen into decline with some of the larger homes having been converted into businesses or divided into rental units. Mayor Olgiati advocated new development along the city's west side, which would come to be known as the Golden Gateway Redevelopment Project (near today's West ML King Boulevard). Despite some opposition, portions of the hill were removed to make way for a new highway and bridge. More than a thousand buildings would have to be torn down, and 1,400 families would have to be relocated. The site was approved in 1954, and the four-year project was underway a year later.

Shortly after the bridge opened to traffic in 1959, it was officially named in honor of the mayor, who was at the peak of his political power. He had just won his third term, and had his eyes on a bigger prize: governor of Tennessee. He ran against incumbent Gov. Buford Ellington in 1962, and lost. Olgiati's fortunes did not improve in the 1963 mayoral race, when 34-

year-old attorney Ralph Kelley unseated him, sending the "boss" into political retirement at the age of 61. He made one more race, for his old Public Works Commissioner post in 1975, but his time had passed.

J.B. Collins said that Olgiati spent much of his later years on a farm in north Georgia, raising Black Angus cattle. He said Olgiati's only son, Charles preceded him in death, "and Rudy was never the same after that. It took a lot of the wind out of him." In the 1980s, after the death of his wife Mae, Olgiati moved to Charleston, South Carolina, to be near his daughter Virginia. It was there he died in 1989, eighteen days shy of his 88th birthday. He is buried at Chattanooga's Forest Hills Cemetery.

His bridge has been widened and expanded a few times over the years, and is now attractive and busy. Call it Ol' Johnny, Ol' Jolly, or anything you like, but give credit to Mr. Olgiati himself for his role in the growth of Chattanooga.

How to Be a Volunteer Bama Dawg

When I was growing up, WDEF-TV called its newscast *Tri-State Report*. I always liked that title, because it was self-explanatory. Folks like me, in the northeastern corner of Alabama, got their news from Chattanooga, as did my neighbors in northwest Georgia, just a skip and a hop away. Somehow over the years, the term "tri-state area" was replaced by "the Tennessee Valley," although I don't know who made that decision. I guess it sounded more tourist-friendly.

Still, I'm proud of our three adjoining states. I love something about all of them. Yet until recently, I never entertained the idea of standing in all three states at the same time. I guess somewhere in the back of my head, I realized there was a border where the three states joined each other. I just never bothered to find out exactly where it was, until now.

My friend Bill Peterson told me I needed to take a hike. He had just returned from a field trip in which he found the marker that commemorates the exact spot where Alabama meets Georgia, which meets Tennessee.

As you know, there was renewed interest in the Tennessee-Georgia border a few years ago. Some Georgia state legislators claimed the state line was marked incorrectly, too far to the south. This had been done in 1818 by James Camak. He was a surveyor, hired by the state of Georgia to settle a dispute over state lines. (Georgia became a state in 1788, while Tennessee established statehood eight years later). Camak, of course, used primitive equipment. As surveyor Bart Crattie told NPR in 2008, the folks in the 1800's used "the heavens and stars" to mark the line.

There seems to be little doubt among modern-day experts that the marker is about a mile off the 35th parallel, which according to legal statute, is the actual line. It should be, they say, right in the middle of Nickajack Lake.

Yes, all that water, just out of Georgia's reach. But as currently drawn, it is a 200-year-old line, and unlikely to budge any time soon.

So in 2013, Georgia lawmakers claimed the true boundary line would enable Georgians to lay claim to Tennessee's abundant water supply. Despite the outcry, and some well-researched evidence that seems to prove them right, the state line hasn't moved. Apparently, the courts are reluctant to start moving state lines that have existed for two hundred years. As surveyor Crattie told NPR, "Lord, if you started changing property lines, it would just be chaos."

In 2005, some interested parties found the spot, and were kind enough to create a small monument, and then drive it into the ground for all to see. The key word is "small," about four inches in diameter.

Considerately, they placed bright orange surveyor's tape on some trees to keep people like me from wandering off the trail. Even with their help, I pretty much stumbled on it, thanks to a white paper towel held in place by a rock. I removed the rock, and there it was!

Standing in three states at once, like a true Volunteer Bama Dawg

For the first time in my life, I was truly a tri-state guy. My left foot was in Tennessee, and the big toe of my right foot was in Georgia. The heel of my right foot was in Alabama. I guess you could say I was a Volunteer Bama Dawg.

The exact spot, at the borders of Marion County, TN,
Jackson County, AL, and Dade County, GA

I was standing in one of only 38 such spots in the USA, where three states are so connected on dry land (23 are in the middle of rivers, streams or lakes). I'm told that more than 200,000 tourists a year visit the Four Corners monument, where the states of Utah, Arizona, New Mexico, and Colorado all meet. Our little spot doesn't have that kind of tourist traffic, but if it ever does, I have first dibs on the souvenir shop.

If you would like to stand in all three states, here are the directions:

From Interstate 24, take exit 161 (Haletown/New Hope). Take TN-156 west (a curvy, winding road) 3.8 miles, then turn left on Macedonia Church Road. Go 7/10 of a mile, then turn right on Huckabee Road (it isn't marked, but it is just before you see several mailboxes on the left). Go 3/10 of a mile and park just beyond the Stateline Cemetery. You'll see the beginning of a trail straight ahead. Walk about 50 yards and you'll see orange surveyors tape on some trees. The marker stands about a foot off the ground, and lies just ahead of a natural stone formation.

Growing Up with Only 3 Channels

I arrived into this world during the Baby Boomer generation. I was one of those privileged children raised by parents who were products of the Great Depression. Hoyt and Ruth Carroll, like others of their era, came up the hard way. Their relatives found cheap land in rural northeast Alabama in the 1930s, so they made their way up Sand Mountain on wagons pulled by horses along rutted, muddy trails. Things didn't really get much better until around the time I was born. It was a lucky coincidence for me.

When I would hear my parents, uncles and aunts recount their tales of growing up in the cotton fields, with no indoor plumbing, and bedrooms shared by their many siblings, I realized how easy I had it by comparison. What would I tell my children some day?

The answer is pretty much what you would expect, coming from me. "Boys, when I was your age, we didn't have remote controls for our TV sets." Looking extra pitiful, I would inform them I had to physically remove myself from the sofa, walk all the way over to the TV, and manually change the channel.

If that didn't garner enough sympathy, I would go one step further. Not only did I have to perform that tiring chore, but there were only THREE channels to choose from. Not thirty, not three hundred, not a thousand. Only three. This was in the 1960s.

Chattanooga's first television station signed on the air in 1954, with a second one arriving in 1956, and finally a third one in 1958. So for viewers of that era, three choices seemed just fine. Until of course, you had to get up and change channels. For the first several years of my life, I served, quite willingly, as my parents' human remote control. I never complained, it got me nearer to TV glory.

In researching my *Chattanooga Radio and Television* book, I learned a lot about the local broadcasters who led the way, back in those early days.

Wayne Abercrombie, who was Channel 3's first employee, helped set up the first live remote broadcasts from theaters, store openings, Lookout Mountain, and even the lake. Back then, it required big trucks, lots of lights, and miles of cable. Now, we do it with a cell phone. Yes, just a cell phone.

Abercrombie also described the early variety shows, set up in a tiny, cramped studio under hot lights. Local TV was largely considered to be radio with pictures back then, and they took it quite literally. It was not uncommon for a host to hold up a copy of *Life* or *Look* magazine, or a book of travel photos, and just hold it up to the camera and flip through the pages while an instrumental record played in the background.

Eventually they enlisted live entertainers. Local singers, musicians and dancers were called upon to help fill the time, and that worked out pretty well, except for one thing. If they called in sick, or got snowed in, the TV host still had an hour-long show to do.

One day, such an occurrence changed the life of a Channel 3 employee, who up until then, had been behind the scenes.

Jimmy Nabors was a 26-year-old native of Sylacauga, Alabama. Back home, he had sung in high school and church, and had acted in a few plays while attending the University of Alabama. To get his foot in the door of a TV station, he took a job at Channel 3 as a film cutter. He was responsible for editing the film from commercials and news stories.

One afternoon, while the daily "Holiday for Housewives" hour was airing, a scheduled guest didn't show up, and the host realized he had several minutes left in the show. He sent an assistant scrambling through the station's offices, asking co-workers if they had any hidden talents. If so, he said, now's your chance. Eventually, he spotted Nabors in the film room. He asked, "Jimmy, is there anything you can do on live TV?" In his natural Alabama drawl he replied, "Well, I can sing" (although that word sounded like "sang" coming out of his mouth).

There was no time to check the accuracy of his claims, so they rushed him into the studio, turned on the lights, handed him the microphone, and crossed their fingers.

Jim Nabors on WRGP-TV Channel 3 in Chattanooga, 1958

What happened next was a TV miracle, the stuff of which legends are made. The film cutter with the high-pitched, twangy accent opened his mouth, and out came the richest, purest baritone they had ever heard. When he finished, everyone looked at each other in amazement, and then looked at Nabors. "Wow, we had no idea, you were absolutely great!" He just smiled back and said, "Well, I told ya I could sang . . ."

It was soon apparent that Nabors' talents were best suited in front of the camera, and after a trip to Hollywood, he never looked back. From the Steve Allen Show, to the Andy Griffith Show, his own show, and concert stages worldwide, Nabors has had a wonderful career. As he proudly told me in a 1994 interview, it all started in Chattanooga.

Long before Nabors, other nationally known entertainers also got their start on Chattanooga broadcasting stations. Sixteen-year-old Georgie Goebel sang and played on WDOD Radio in the 1930s before becoming George Gobel on national TV a couple of decades later. Archie Campbell was playing a character named "Grandpappy" on the same station at age 22, thirty years before going national on "Hee Haw."

Before videotaping eliminated the need to do everything live, Nashville performers circled their way around the Southeast each week, doing live programs in Chattanooga and other TV markets. Flatt & Scruggs, Bill Anderson, Arthur Smith and others parked their buses outside the local stations once a week to pick, grin, and sell corn meal and cough medicine.

Porter Wagoner and his crew made a weekly stop at Channel 3 for several years in the 1960s, unloading their gear for a thirty-minute show each week before heading to the next town.

Dolly Parton was a member of Porter Wagoner's traveling troupe in the 1960s.

Channel 3's original studio, at 1214 McCallie Avenue, didn't have much space, but they used every available inch to squeeze Wagoner's band into camera range. Longtime fans will remember that Wagoner always had a "girl singer," and for several years it was Dolly Parton. Station employees still laugh as they recall tiny Miss Parton rushing into the closet-sized dressing room with a box "as big as she was," they say, which contained her larger-than-life wig.

In the early days of local TV, several radio announcers were invited to try their hand at this new medium of TV. Most were hired, and assigned, by the quality of their voice. Deep-voiced guys like Mort Lloyd were asked to read the news, sports enthu-siasts covered the ball games, and the best ad-libbers were as-signed to do the weather.

At that time, of course, there was no technology involved in TV weather forecasting. Today, my colleague Paul Barys has a degree in meteorology and an arsenal of computers and radar devices at his disposal. But in the 1950s, the weatherman would drive to the airport, get the best guess from the meteorologist on duty, and then return to the station to start marking "highs" and "lows" on the national weather map.

Eventually, some of the weather guys seized the opportunity to make their segment the lighter, happier part of the newscast. Harve Bradley, who did the weather on Channel 12, was a witty fellow who never took his job that seriously. He was not above having someone sprinkle paper snowflakes on his head if snow was in the forecast. If he had happened to make an errant pre-diction the day before, he would return the next day, look into the camera and say, "Folks, do you really think I can predict the weather in Chattanooga? Look out your window. Do you see those mountains? No one can predict the weather in this town!"

He also unapologetically admitted he could not identify every single state on the United States map, often referring to Wyoming or Colorado as "one of those square states."

One of Harve's best moments came during a time of great technological advance. The station had purchased a magnetic weather board, allowing him to place little lightning bolts and snowflakes on the map.

As he was presenting his forecast on live TV, he was about to talk about the chances of snow, when the snowflake magnet fell to the floor. Without missing a beat, he said, "We might get a little snow, but as you can see, it's not going to stick."

It Can't Get Any Better Than This!

On April 13, 1925, Chattanooga started broadcasting and has never stopped. WDOD-AM became the city's first radio station. At first, it was on just three nights a week, for 90 minutes a night. In the 1930s, programming was expanded: they hired musical entertainers, plus a morning host.

By the 1940s, there were three radio stations in town, all of them affiliated with major radio networks. Listeners heard live reports from the front lines of World War II, providing an immediacy that newspapers could not deliver. No doubt, folks were impressed by this major technological advance.

Then came the 1950s. WDEF Channel 12 became the area's first TV station, which was great for merchants who were trying to sell televisions. By the end of the decade, the number of local channels had tripled. There were now so many choices. It surely couldn't get any better than that.

In the 1960s, AM radio stations ruled the airwaves. That decade also brought us "living color," and if you were the first person in your neighborhood to have a color TV, you had plenty of visitors enjoying "Walt Disney's Wonderful World of Color." It was also the decade when TV news became more than just a guy reading at a desk. By then, news teams were filming their stories, and could usually get the film developed and on the air the very same day!

In the 1970s, Chattanooga had more radio stations than ever, and the FM band was emerging as the preferred choice. But radio had to deal with a new form of competition: 8-track tapes. Now, we could listen to the songs we liked, without being dictated by a radio station. By the end of the decade, the music tapes got even smaller, as cassettes became popular. Wow, twelve songs inside a little rectangular case. It would never get any more compact than that, right?

As the 1980s began, some of us had cable, or satellite TV, and we were able to watch thirty channels! We had one for music, one for sports, and we could even buy jewelry on a shopping channel. One channel, CNN put the news on 24 hours a day. "How could they possibly fill all that time?" we wondered.

As for music, we had compact discs now. No more tapes to rewind or break. Those flat little CD's would hold more than an hour of music, and we were convinced that it would never get better than that.

By the 1990s, TV stations had satellite trucks, enabling newscasters to bounce their signal toward the heavens, and broadcast from just about anywhere. In addition to our local channels, we had about a hundred more from around the world. This was the decade that dial-up Internet moved into our living rooms, along with a big fat monitor, a tall computer tower, and a noisy printer. Eventually, local news outlets would set up on the worldwide web, and our sources for information were rapidly multiplying. Some of us started carrying a wireless mobile phone, which was about the size and weight of a brick.

By the 2000s, those cell phones started getting smaller, and most of them doubled as a camera! Many of us now had high-speed Internet, and those old-timey CD's had been replaced by iPods, which put thousands of songs in our pockets, directly connected to our ears. We hung out together on Facebook, at least when we weren't texting or Tweeting.

Now the TV screens in our home are bigger than ever. Still, we strain to watch videos, read the news, and even enjoy a book on our tiny mobile screens, at least until the battery dies. Recharging our device's battery ranks right up there with food, drink, and sleep as a personal necessity, especially when traveling. Oh, and by the way, TV reporters now use those little phones to transmit live segments you see on the news. The gas-guzzling satellite trucks are rapidly becoming extinct.

Technology can't possibly get any better, faster, and smaller than it is now. Or can it?

It's the Jet-FLI Spectacular!

What if you turned on your radio today, and heard this announcement: "Coming Saturday to the local auditorium! See the hottest acts in the world, all performing their hits LIVE on stage! Katy Perry! Justin Timberlake! Maroon 5! Blake Shelton! Bruno Mars! Adele! TWO great shows, this Saturday, at 5 and 8 p.m.! Tickets are on sale now for $20!"

That is so ridiculous, right? I mean, ticket prices for any of those acts would be astronomical. Plus, there's no way any one of them would share the stage with any of the others. With all those egos involved, who would open the show? Who would close? And their styles of music are so different. Any promoter would be crazy to put them on the same bill. Besides, no music fan could possibly like them all. It simply would not work.

Yet in the 1960s, it did work. Ask any baby boomer who grew up in Chattanooga about the *Jet-FLI Spectaculars*, and they will tell you some stories, outrageous stories. On any given night, more than half of the acts in Billboard's Top Ten would be on the same stage, one right after another. Tickets ranged from $2.50 to $3.50.

WFLI Spectacular *print ad from 1968. Check out those ticket prices.*

If you missed Paul Revere and the Raiders this year, they just might be back next year. Same goes for Herman's Hermits and other repeat visitors.

At the time, WFLI was a powerful AM Top 40 station. Its strong signal captured most of the young adult audience of the Baby Boomer generation. WFLI was among a group of stations owned in part by the Brennan family of Alabama. The others were in Birmingham, Montgomery, and Jacksonville, Florida. The family pooled its resources to create multi-star shows twice a year in each city, making it convenient for the artists. For example, they'd schedule shows Friday in Chattanooga, Saturday in Birmingham and Sunday in Montgomery, so the artists had an easier flight schedule.

Ticket prices were low, according to WFLI's first general manager Johnny Eagle, to allow as many people as possible to come. "It wasn't meant to be a money-maker," he said. "Our owner just wanted to promote the radio station, and boy did it ever work!" The first Spectacular was staged on March 19, 1965, and for the next six years, the shows were guaranteed sellouts. Listeners anxiously awaited the announcements of the lineups for the summer and winter shows. The deejays would promote about five acts for a few weeks, and then just before the show, a "surprise special guest" would be added. With great fanfare, they would tell us that Johnny Rivers or Andy Kim or some other big name "has just been added . . . you'd better get your tickets now!"

Incredibly, in that pre-Internet era, ticket sales were handled one by one, by the WFLI staff. People sent cash in self-addressed, stamped envelopes, or drove to the studio to get them in person. "We handled everything, from setting up the sound, hiring the security, making travel arrangements, and getting the stars to and from the airport," Eagle said. Peter Noone and Herman's Hermits got here three days early in the summer of 1967, and they had a great time waterskiing at Lake Chickamauga."

It didn't always go smoothly. A few days before a heavily promoted 1966 show, Eagle heard about some confusion involving Paul Revere and the Raiders. They had the number-one song in the nation, and were outselling the Beatles. But the Raiders had mistakenly booked two shows in Atlanta on the same day as the WFLI shows. "We freaked out," Eagle said. "Nobody wanted to go on stage and tell five thousand screaming kids that the Raiders were no-shows. We arranged for our co-owner in Birmingham to take his private jet to Atlanta, pick up the Raiders after their 3:00 show, fly them to Chattanooga in time to open our 5:30 show, fly them back to Atlanta to open their 8:00 show, and then fly them back here to close our 9:00 show. We paid police escorts to get them to and from the airport twice, and hired a crew to haul their gear on and off the stage, every time."

If that wasn't enough, Eagle said, "Jan and Dean threw a fit that night. They thought they were the headliners, and insisted on closing the second show. We told them the Raiders would be arriving late, and they would have to be the last act. Jan and Dean argued with us all evening, threatening not to go on. Nobody follows us, they said. We had to stall for time, sending some deejays out at intermission to tell the crowd we were having technical difficulties. Actually it was just Jan and Dean being a giant pain in the butt!" Eventually the duo gave in, after being told they wouldn't get paid if they didn't play.

The falsetto-voiced Lou Christie ("Lightning Strikes") caused a different kind of problem. "He turned the gals on," Eagle said. "He would rip off his shirt, but that was considered racy back then. It would get the girls too excited. He did it at the 5:30 show, and the police told us if he did it again at 9:00, they would close the curtains."

On another occasion, Jerry Lee Lewis lived up to his bad-boy reputation. Eagle said, "His career had cooled off, but he was still Jerry Lee. He didn't want second billing to anyone. We got Neil Diamond, and he was a bigger name at the time, so he was our headliner. Jerry Lee raised hell of course, but I think it was just for the sake of raising hell."

Not every act caused a headache. Eagle speaks fondly of Roy Orbison. "He just stood there on stage, didn't say much and didn't move a muscle, but he sure could sing. The girls loved his voice, and the guys loved his guitar playing."

Rick Govan, known as "Ringo Van, the Music Man" during his radio days, worked at WFLI while attending the University of Chattanooga in the '60s. He said, "I think back and realize how lucky I was to chat backstage with Lesley Gore, to drive Lou Christie to the airport with all those star-struck girls following us, and to see Jerry Lee Lewis throwing a tantrum. Yes, those are wonderful memories indeed. Sometimes I wish I could turn back the hands of time. For a college kid, it was a wild ride. Like the Troggs sang in their big hit 'Wild Thing,' it was . . . groovy."

CHAPTER 9

Gone, But Not Forgotten

Dalton Roberts: Man of Many Talents

Dalton Roberts, as illustrated by W.C. King in 1980

How many hats did Dalton Roberts wear? Guitar picker. Teacher. Politician. Songwriter. Storyteller. Poet. County Executive. Newspaper columnist. Friend to the birds. Singer. Tax-dollar watchdog. BS detector. Visionary.

Dalton passed away in December 2015. He'd been in failing health for a while. As he told a friend at his favorite barber shop shortly before his death, "I just ain't doing no good. Everything seems to be falling apart." As Dalton struggled to put one foot in front of the other, we didn't see him much anymore. The music was silenced and the writing ceased. Still, it wouldn't have surprised anyone if he had come roaring back like a lion. Now we're left with only memories of an unforgettable man.

He packed a lot of life into 82 years, didn't he? He'd be the first to tell you, and he frequently did, that he was the product of good parents. Roy and Nora Roberts were opposites in many ways, and kindred spirits in others. Roy was a man of few words, and some said that was because Nora used them all. Dalton was a great mix of the two. He had his dad's sly humor and work ethic, and his mom's love of reading and FDR-inspired Democratic advocacy.

Dalton was a frequent guest on my TV shows, and what a blessing he was. On a slow news day, my boss would say, "David, can you find a story to fill some time?" I'd call Dalton and say, "Do you wanna get something off your chest about Erlanger Hospital?" He'd respond, "Bring that camera over to my office, and I'll give you some news." The hospital's CEO at that time was Tom Winston. Dalton was infuriated by the hospital's high executive salaries, and its agreement to accept infectious waste from other hospitals. Winston would choose his words carefully when challenged by the loquacious County Executive, and soon learned what the rest of us already knew: you don't win a war of words with Dalton Roberts.

Anyone who blames a lack of education on a poor upbringing should study the life of Dalton Roberts. His family didn't have much, for sure. But he read every book he could get his hands on. It used to be fun to watch dual public appearances featuring Dalton and the other local leader of that era named Roberts: Gene, the mayor of Chattanooga. Dalton grew up in a Chattanooga community called The Watering Trough. Gene grew up a few miles away in Onion Bottom. They would try to "out-poor" each other. Although they had vastly different styles, both were well-read, articulate leaders. Neither ever lost an election.

You can read elsewhere about Dalton's massive list of achievements, resulting in the development of the Trade Center, the Tennessee Riverpark, Enterprise South, and so much more. It's obvious that at the end of his 16 years at the helm of Hamilton County government, he left it in much better shape than he found it. I want to focus on one Dalton Roberts story that sums up this very impressive man.

In 2012, Dalton was slowing down physically, but would still tell stories, pick and sing when he was invited to do so. A ladies' library club in north Georgia hosted Dalton at its monthly luncheon. During the business portion of the meeting, the club president shared some bad news about the library's decreasing revenues.

A few minutes later, Dalton was introduced. He greeted the audience, sat on the stool and started in with some stories and songs. The library ladies loved his show, rewarding him with laughter and applause. Like a lot of entertainers, when he finished his show, he held up his latest CD. "If y'all like those songs," he drawled, "I brought some CDs to sell. They're twenty bucks each, and I'd be honored if you'd take one home with you."

The audience lined up to shake hands with Dalton, get his autograph, and buy his CD. It's what happened next that I'll never forget. After Dalton had shaken every hand and sold every CD, he grabbed the stack of twenty-dollar bills, walked over to the club president and said, "Here, this money's for the library. I know you'll put it to good use."

That kind gesture didn't make the news. Dalton didn't do it to get attention. It's just another example of a man who loved words, music and good deeds, and still inspires us all to do the same.

MaryEllen Locher: Her Name Lives On

MaryEllen Locher in the 1990s

I never got to know WTVC Chattanooga news anchor MaryEllen Locher as well as I would have liked. In the world of local TV news, those of us who work as Channel 3 anchors see each other every day. I've seen Cindy Sexton and Paul Barys thousands of times over the years, day in and day out. There just aren't many opportunities to mingle with "the competition."

I first met "Mel," as her friends called her, at the Riverbend Festival in 1988. She was friendly, and of course quite beautiful. I found out that she and my wife Cindy had Penn State in common, before both moved south for broadcasting jobs. After that, I only saw her a handful of times in person, including her wedding and that of a co-worker or two. Again, she was always friendly, always beautiful.

Like every other news viewer in Chattanooga, I would occasionally notice her absence from the Channel 9 anchor desk, often for weeks at a time. When one is on TV each day, there are no secrets, and soon it became public knowledge that Mel was battling cancer. She was barely thirty when she was first diagnosed. It came and it went a few times over the years, and for long stretches we were hopeful she had beaten the disease. But as is too often the case, it would return with a vengeance.

Mel's life ended at the age of 45, on June 9, 2005. She was survived by a loving husband, a young son, and thousands of friends. This was in the pre-Facebook era, so these were real friends, not virtual ones. They had hung on every word about her condition, they had sent her cards, and they had donated comfortable and stylish hats for fellow cancer patients ("Hats from the Heart," one of Mel's pet causes). I was particularly touched by this excerpt from her obituary: *"It is not often in this life that one is blessed to be touched by someone whose very presence shines a ray of hope and faith to the darkest corners of the world around her."* That is so true.

Her longtime co-anchor Bob Johnson was among the speakers at her memorial service. He paid tribute to "My good friend, my buddy. She had such a good heart." He told me that in the male-dominated newsroom of the 1980s, "She was one of the guys. She could tell a joke; she could take a joke. No big ego, no pretensions. She was just a smart, fun lady."

When I visit clubs and churches about my Chattanooga Radio/TV book, I show a few photos on the big screen, and MaryEllen's photo always makes folks tear up a bit. When you invite someone into your home, night after night, they're like family. When MaryEllen left us, we lost a friend. We sure were proud when she devoted so much of her time to causes that would help others in their personal battles. She was a founding member of Chattanooga's Make-A-Wish Foundation, which has helped so many ailing young people see their dreams come true.

Today, her name lives on, as it will forever at Memorial Hospital's MaryEllen Locher Breast Center. The people who established it, and who run it today, are committed to excellence. My wife tells me those who work there are especially good at people skills, making visitors feel comfortable.

Established in 2007, the center meets MaryEllen's original vision of making the breast cancer journey easier for all women. Working alongside Memorial Hospital, she provided insight and inspiration for the development of a breast center that would combine the best possible medical care in an atmosphere of calm and understanding. Reducing the time between diagnosis and treatment was her primary goal.

It's a great tribute to have your name attached to a health care facility with a solid reputation. Mel deserves only the best.

David Earl Hughes: Larger Than Life

On August 22, 2004, my radio friend Dex called me at home. It was late that Sunday afternoon, and when I heard his voice, I knew it wasn't good news.

"David Earl Hughes just died," Dex said. David had just turned 48, and was in the prime of his career.

David Earl defined the term "larger than life." About ten years earlier, a fellow US-101 deejay also died suddenly, and young. He too, was overweight and didn't take very good care of himself. "That's it, I've gotta clean up my act," David said. And for a while, he did. But old habits are hard to break, and he resumed his regular lifestyle until his heart could no longer take it.

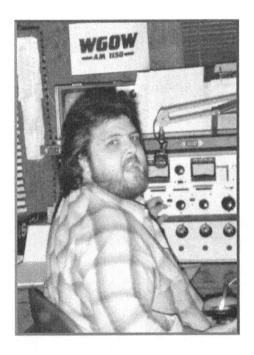

David Earl Hughes at WGOW in 1980

I first met David when he was on Chattanooga's WGOW in 1980. I was on KZ-106 two doors down the hall, and he started his midday shift as I was ending my morning show, around 10:00 a.m. each day. He made an immediate connection with listeners with his booming bass voice and distinctive drawl. He was proudly Southern to the core, and he delighted in baiting "Yankees" like my then-girlfriend (now wife) Cindy. It was fun watching them go at it. She wouldn't back down, and he liked that.

In 1985, a couple of years after I left KZ-106, the station wanted to create a different kind of morning show, modeled after the *Morning Zoo* format in other parts of the country. The KZ programmers recruited David Earl from WGOW, and moved up "Jammer" Jay Scott from the night show to create their own Morning Zoo. Other station personalities rounded out the cast, and the KZ Morning Zoo resulted in chaos and high ratings for about five years.

During that time, I would still see David each weekend at our *Foul Tips* radio team softball games, and he would tell me about offers from stations in bigger markets, even Chicago. But he seemed to prefer country music, and his goal was to eventually work in Nashville. In 1990, he got an offer from Chattanooga's top radio station, country music giant US-101, and he was released from the Zoo.

Getting the afternoon show at US-101 turned into a great career move. He was right at home from day one, and he took their already-strong ratings even higher. A few years later, he did a very admirable and generous thing. Bill Poindexter, better known as "Dex," had started in local radio before going into national record promotion. He had tired of the constant travel. He settled back into his north Georgia home, and had taken a couple of retail jobs to tide him over. He soon realized how much he missed radio, and he convinced US-101 to give him a job, any job, to get his foot back in the door. They assigned him to set up remote broadcasts, and do traffic reports.

On many days, he reported traffic on David Earl's afternoon show, and the two built up a great rapport. Their personalities meshed well. Each could make the other laugh, and they had natural chemistry. I'll pause here to say that 99% of radio hosts enjoy being solo. Think of Howard Stern. He is surrounded by co-hosts and sidekicks, who make up a huge part of his show. But his show never was, and never will be called "Howard and Robin," or "Howard and Jackie." The same goes for Dan Patrick, Tom Joyner and many others. There's only one "star" of their shows. David Earl wasn't like that. He knew his show was better when Dex was trading one-liners with him. Almost immediately, this one-man, top-rated afternoon radio show became "Dave and Dex." A very good show became a great one. Just like that, Dave and Dex were a team.

In addition to their witty banter, they also became well-known for a radio rarity. Against all conventional wisdom, they set aside part of their Wednesday afternoon shows for "Church Songs." At Dave's insistence, this top-ranked country station took a weekly break from the usual drinkin' and cheatin' songs to play Southern Gospel quartet music most big radio stations wouldn't touch. It only made their show more popular.

The duo scored some astronomical ratings, but in 2003, David Earl's dream job opened up: the afternoon show at powerful country station WSM-FM in Nashville. The biggest, deepest voice in country radio had a chance to be heard every day in Music City, by those who were making the music. At first, Dave and Dex were going as a team, but Dex decided to stay in Chattanooga. David Earl didn't want to uproot his family, so he made the daily two-hour commute, which had to be tiring. His tenure in Nashville was destined to be brief, cut short by his death a year later at age 48.

We all have our David Earl stories. When our KZ-106 Foul Tips softball team visited neighboring towns, big Dave was a crowd favorite. He played first base (making a great target for our infielders). Occasionally he would wear overalls, or his own size XXXL jersey, with number 747 on the back. It looked just right on him, and it was always good for a laugh.

US-101 station manager Sammy George joined Dex as the main speakers at David Earl's memorial service. In addition to the great stories and hymns, the musicians played the theme from his favorite TV series, "The Andy Griffith Show." David Earl wouldn't have had it any other way.

We'll Always Love Luther

Luther Masingill in 1976

On October 20, 2014, we lost Luther Masingill, at the age of 92. He would no longer speak into the WDEF microphone, attempting to find lost dogs. He was on the same time, same station since 1940. When you see a list of records that will never be broken (like Cal Ripken's consecutive game streak and Joe DiMaggio's 56-game hitting streak), Luther's longevity should rank at the very top.

Take it from me, or anyone else who's ever worked on radio or television. An announcing career, to put it kindly, is not one where many folks get a gold watch for 25 years of continuous service. Deejays come and go, and frequently come again. Chattanooga, being a mid-sized city, has long been considered a stepping stone to Nashville, Atlanta, or even network fame. Generally, if you haven't hit the big time by the time you're middle-aged, you start selling real estate, or get a job at the post office, or start your own business. You can't be a Chattanooga radio announcer forever. Unless you're Luther.

Each year, I attend a reunion of local radio deejays, from past and present. Sometimes we ask them to name the stations for which they've worked, and that can be time-consuming for some. One year, when it was Luther's turn, I fed him a straight line. "Luther," I said, "you've done radio for more than seventy years. How many stations have you worked for?" With impeccable timing, he paused, started looking at his fingers as if to begin counting, looked up and said simply, "One," to great laughter of course.

I also asked him the question people often ask me. When I've touted Luther to out-of-towners, they'll ask, "If he's so good, why didn't he ever make it to the big time?" You see, Chattanooga may seem like a big deal to those of us who live here, but big-city folk are not impressed. We don't have big-league sports, we don't have 16-lane highways and we're not swarming with celebrities. So, if you haven't worked your way out of our scenic little town, you can't be very good, so they say.

After a little prodding, Luther admitted that during his heyday in the 1950s and '60s, he could have gone just about anywhere. As television gradually connected our nation from coast to coast, Easterners became infatuated with Southern-style entertainers. Suddenly, New York-type stars like Milton Berle, Sid Caesar and Groucho Marx were giving way to Southern comics and singers: Dinah Shore, Andy Griffith, Jimmy Dean, Tennessee Ernie Ford and Pat Boone were all near the top of the popularity charts. Big city radio stations took notice. "Hmmm," they said. "Maybe we should hire a down-home Southern deejay to do our morning show." When they saw Luther's eye-popping ratings, they tracked him down.

After all, he was the guy who made an entire city pull over to the side of the road one morning. As heavy snow began to fall, Luther advised his listeners to let some air out of their tires to gain more traction. As witnesses would later describe, main arteries like McCallie Avenue came to a standstill as motorists stopped, got out of their car and began deflating their tires. Can you imagine anyone, in any broadcast medium, having that sort of influence today?

Yet despite the offers from New York, Philadelphia and Milwaukee, Luther chose to stay put. His family was in Chattanooga, and he always appreciated WDEF for giving an unproven high school senior a job on the radio, which was beyond his wildest dreams. When he applied, all he wanted to do was answer the phone and take requests for the older guys.

Radio station owner Joe Engel had met the teenager at Bill Penney Service Station on Dodds Avenue. He heard Luther's voice on the intercom system ("Mr. Engel, your car is ready"), and asked him to try out for an announcer's job. Luther drove to the station's downtown studio, where he was given a commercial script to read. He mispronounced one word ("salon" became "saloon") but those golden pipes landed him a job, and he quickly moved up the ladder. By the way, if the 74-year radio gig isn't impressive enough, consider this: he was also on WDEF Channel 12 every day since it signed on, in April of 1954. No one else in the nation could claim that distinction, either.

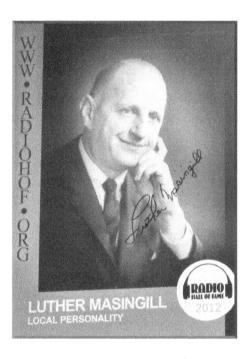

Commemorating Luther Masingill's induction into the
National Radio Hall of Fame in Chicago, 2012

In his later years, he received some long-overdue attention. There was a stretch of highway named in his honor, he was
among the first inductees into the Tennessee Radio Hall of
Fame, and he was inducted into the National Radio Hall of
Fame in Chicago. Accompanied by friends, family, colleagues
and competitors, he was resplendent in his tuxedo, accepting
the award from fellow Hall of Famer Ralph Emery.

At the time of the national honor, he had just turned 90. The
Chicago trip was invigorating for Luther, yet tiring as well. Late
that Saturday night, as he was receiving friends in the hotel
lobby, I recounted his recent honors. "Luther, you've been honored by the city, the state, the Tennessee Radio Hall of Fame,
the National Hall of Fame," and I was just getting warmed up.

I continued, "You know, I think we can get you honored at the White House." I was serious, sort of.

He looked at me, wagged his finger, shook his head, and said, "David . . . you'd better not!" He was serious. I think he'd had all the honors, and tuxedo fittings he could stand.

At unveiling of Luther Masingill Parkway on South Broad Street in Chattanooga, 2010

During his final years, I was fortunate to spend more time with him. We spent a good bit of time together at book signings, speaking engagements, or just lunch. Everywhere he went, someone thanked him for waking them up, for reuniting them with their pet, or for finding their car keys. Luther knew he was loved, and nothing made him happier than rising bright and early, driving to the studio so he could help someone have a better day.

Every time I saw or heard Luther, I cherished the moment. This much is certain: there will never be another one like him, anywhere in the world.

Dear Luther: Just One More Thing

*Celebration of Life for Luther Masingill, Engel Stadium
in Chattanooga, October 23, 2014*

I never got to tell Luther goodbye. I wish I'd had that chance. This is what I would have told him.

Dear Luther:

It's just beginning to sink in. I checked my calendar for next week. For Monday, I had written a note a few weeks ago: "Call Luther," to see if you would go with me Friday to speak to the Brainerd Kiwanis Club. It won't be the same.

We sure had fun together! I've made so many speeches about Chattanooga radio and TV, and I sang your praises every time. Often, you were with me, and people were so happy when I brought a special guest: The Longest Running Broadcaster in the History of the

World! You got a standing ovation every time.

I'm glad we shared some long car rides. I learned so much about you during those rides. Once, I knew you weren't feeling well, so we talked about life and death. You asked about my parents, who you met decades ago. I told you about my Dad's "Celebration of Life," and how we honored his memory with humor and upbeat stories. You told me, "Yeah, I hope y'all do that for me too . . ."

I remembered that, when I got the sad phone call about you early that day. I'd heard you were ailing. I had visited you in the hospital in years past, and you always bounced back. Why should this time be any different?

Then came the day I knew would come. Or maybe I really didn't. You'll laugh when I tell you this, but here you are, a 92-year-old man who has been seriously ill a few times in the past couple of years, and I was totally unprepared when I heard the news. All my "Luther memorabilia" was scattered everywhere, and all those taped interviews we did were all over the place. You spoiled me, old pal!

Let me tell you about the first lesson you taught me: you didn't even know you did it. One morning early in my radio career, I was having a bad day. Some of the equipment wasn't working properly, and I was in a bad mood. Evidently, it was affecting my on-air performance. My station manager at the time (your former boss Jerry Lingerfelt) came in and asked me what was wrong. I started complaining about the equipment, figuring he would understand why I was grouchy. He said, "Have you ever heard Luther sound angry?" I answered honestly, "No he always sounds the same." "Right," Jerry said. "He always sounds cheerful. Do you think his equipment works perfectly every day?" "Uh, no," I said sheepishly. "Right," Jerry said. "Think about that for a while." I never forgot that. Lesson learned.

I'm sure you heard my tribute to you at Engel Stadium. It was at least ten minutes too long, but there was so much to say. One of my co-workers told me the next day, "I never got to meet Luther, but after listening to you, I feel like I knew him." That made me feel good, because that was my goal.

I know, I'm getting long-winded again. I just wanted you to know I'm thinking of you. I saw your name on my phone, and I will never delete it. Why should I? Just seeing the name "Luther" makes me smile. Even though you've moved outside my coverage area, I can still hear your voice. I noticed that I had not erased a 2012 voice mail message from you. I played it back just to see why I had saved it.

You finished the message by saying, "Thanks David. I love you. You're a good guy."

I wonder if I've ever left a message for anyone that was so meaningful, it was never erased. I don't think I have. I'm still learning from you, old pal. Now go have some laughs with your friends, hug all those dogs you found, and play some Sinatra records.

Love, David

Remembering Luther, a Year Later

Saying goodbye to my friend Luther as he was leaving a radio reunion in 2013

On Monday, October 20, 2014, I woke up and did my daily routine. First, I look at my phone. I check e-mails, messages, Twitter and Facebook. Most days I find I didn't miss anything important.

But that morning, there was a message from Danny Howard, the manager at Sunny 92.3, WDEF radio. Danny used to invite me to fill in for Luther Masingill during his infrequent illnesses and vacations. Danny informed me that Luther had passed away overnight, and asked me to come to the studio to reminisce about his life. Of course, I said "I'm on the way," before realizing I should probably shower and get dressed. In reality, I'm pretty sure I just stood around and processed it for a few minutes.

For most of his life, he had an incredible run of good health. From back in the 1940s, all the way to 2002, he never called in sick. He loved his job so much, he often came in when he was under the weather. After he turned 80, he would get sick now and then, and his wife Mary would insist he stay home. But he was what coaches would call a "gamer." When his number was called, he stepped up to the plate.

He had beaten a couple of serious illnesses in the year before his death, and that may be why I was so surprised when I heard the bad news. In April 2013, he had a urinary tract infection, which is painful and often fatal for elderly patients. I visited him in the hospital, and he was responsive, but weak. Upon leaving, I remember thinking that might be the last time I'd see him. Amazingly, a week later he was back on radio and TV.

Two months later, in June 2013, he was back in the hospital, this time with pneumonia. Again, at age 91, this was very serious. During this visit, he looked even weaker than he did in April. He was not as responsive, and honestly, I was sure I'd seen him for the last time. Well, you guessed it. A few days later he was back at work. So you can't blame me for thinking he could beat just about anything.

As it happened, the following month, I was scheduled to do a program about my Chattanooga Radio & TV book at the Tennessee Valley Theater in Spring City, Tennessee. The owner had asked me to put together a show with some pictures, video and jokes to entertain a theater audience. Although I had taken Luther to some events, I ruled this one out due to his recent health problems.

About two weeks prior to the show date, he called me. "David," he said, "I got a flyer in the mail, and it says you'll be doing a show in Spring City on July 17. Would you like for me to go with you?" Of course I would, if he was able. He loved the stories and the memories, and the audiences loved him. I would set up his jokes, and he delivered the punch lines with his great timing. "Luther?" I'd say, "Are you still doing your exercises?" "Absolutely," he'd reply. "Every morning, I touch the tips of my shoes fifty times." "Really?" I'd say. "Yes sir," he would reply. "Then I take those shoes off the dresser and put 'em on my feet." I heard that one a few hundred times, and he made people laugh every time.

Anyway, when he asked about the Spring City show, I cautioned him, "It's about fifty miles away, and it's late on a Saturday night. Are you sure you'll feel up to it?" "I'll tell you what," he said. "Call me that morning, and I'll see how I feel."

So I did. Around 10 o'clock that morning, I called him. "Luther, the Spring City show is tonight. Do you feel like going?" He said, "Call me back in about ten minutes, I'm buying a new lawnmower." I figured that was a good sign. You don't buy a new lawnmower unless you plan to be around a while!

He bought his lawnmower, worked in his yard, and went along for the ride to Spring City. We had a great time. He did all of his jokes, gave away some prizes, and posed for dozens of pictures. I'm glad I got to spend that evening with Luther. To this day, every time I mention his name to an audience, everyone smiles. How's that for a great legacy?

CHAPTER 10

Laugh Lines and Thank You Notes

You Can't Make This Stuff Up

The best part of my day is calling the computer repair customer service line, and the rep says, "Well, this may take a while. Our computers are running slow today."

I keep getting mail from my former Internet provider, enticing me with discounts and sweet deals to get me back. If they had paid this much attention to me when I was their customer, I wouldn't have left them in the first place.

Here are some of my favorite recent typos, or as we call them now, Auto-Correct bloopers. Or maybe they're really just typos. Anyway, here goes:

"If those idiots raise our taxes again, we should go to the poles to vote those out!"

"I can't believe they didn't close schools today. They need to fire the Super Attendant!"

Speaking of school leaders, one person wrote, "I hope they choose the right one this time. The steaks are really high."

From Facebook: "My son likes rap music, but I think it's just a faze he's going through."

And, "I can't believe how those football players act. They're not good row models."

In the days before AutoCorrect, I got a letter from a promoter asking me if I would have a guy who called himself The Singing Cowboy on my morning show. However, he made a spelling mistake on just one little letter. He wrote, "The Sinning Cowboy." Actually, that might have been way more interesting.

I seem to always find the shopping cart with the bad wheel. The one that feels like you're pushing a Ford F-150. If they held an Olympics for finding the shopping cart with the most wobbly wheels, I'd win the Gold Medal.

You know you're getting old when kids think "Mr. Bojangles" is the guy who runs those chicken restaurants.

True story: Some folks in California found a crumpled bag of baseball cards in a house, valued at $1 million. At our house we moved a recliner, and I found three Skittles, a pencil, and some Cheerios. Plus, a never-returned DVD that probably led to Blockbuster's demise.

There's nothing like being in the dentist's chair. They're poking around in your mouth, and then "OUCH!" you jump and scream. They always ask: "Did that hurt?"

One night, in the cold of winter, I asked my wife if she would get up early the next day, and cook me a hot breakfast. She said there would be a two-hour delay.

I dreamed I was on a romantic vacation with Martha Stewart and my dog. That is so ridiculous. I don't even own a dog.

My wife and I are getting ready for the next presidential debate. It's sure to be another night of finger-pointing, shouting, and insults. Then we'll turn on the TV and watch the candidates.

I have spent approximately 11.2 years of my life on the phone with customer service reps in India, going through various exercises while trying to revive my ailing computers. I have entered codes, inserted discs, and stood on my head while singing the National Anthem. Nothing they've suggested has worked. The only thing that EVER works, is unplugging the device, and then plugging it in again. Yes, the "reboot" is the cure for all malfunctions. So I have revised my will. My wife now knows that if I'm ever plugged into a life support machine, and the doctors say, "We've tried everything, it's too late," she is to personally unplug me, and then plug me back in. I should be good as new, in no time.

I was sitting at the restaurant, looking at the menu. The waitress took my order. The owner came by and said to the waitress, "Did you tell him how excited we were to have a celebrity eat here?" I said, "Come on now, I'm really not that big a deal." "Oh, not you," she said. "Coach Phil Fulmer was here last week."

While getting dressed one morning, I spent at least two minutes looking for my belt, before realizing, I was already wearing it. This is why you trust me to bring you the news.

My Thank You List

I've included several stories about my personal and professional heroes, and I hope they know how much they have meant to me. I could never hope to name everyone and everything that is close to my heart, but since it's the end of the book, this is a good place to send out some special thank-you notes.

Vince, Chris, Cindy, and me having some good food, and lots of laughs

Thank you to the Cindys in my life. Cindy Carroll is my wonderful wife, and the mother of our two great sons. She is also responsible for my new tattoo. You'll have to watch closely to spot it. She also makes my stories better by correcting the mistakes, making me seem smarter than I really am.

Speaking of those two great sons, *thank you*, Chris and Vince. The party started the moment you guys arrived, and it has never stopped. You both make me proud.

Thanks to you, I know I'll leave the world a better place than I found it. That is a great feeling.

Cindy Sexton and me back in 1991. One of us hasn't changed a bit.

Meanwhile, Cindy Sexton joins me in making up the longest-running news anchor team in Tennessee. I can sum up our partnership in two words: Lucky me. *Thank you,* Cindy.

Thank you, Charles Osgood. You lowered my blood pressure every Sunday Morning on CBS. You proved the news can be delivered without theatrics and sensationalism.

Thank you to my late sister Brenda, who loved me and overlooked my flaws since Day One. If you ever have a chance to be the baby of the family, I highly recommend it.

Thank you to those of you who turn your headlights on when driving in rainy or foggy conditions. The rest of you, I worry about.

Thank you to those who faithfully read my blog, newspaper column, Tweets and Facebook posts. I truly appreciate those of you who "get" me. Not everyone does.

My sister, Elaine, also known as a teacher and principal to thousands of kids. I couldn't be any prouder of her.

Thank you to my wonderful sister, Elaine, who is a shining light in my life, and in the lives of so many others. Simply put, you are the best human being I have ever known. Plus, you gave me the world's best nieces, Angela and Anita.

Thank you, Burger King, for being there for me every Monday. You get my week off to a good start.

Thank you, Garry Mac, for being the brother I never had.

Thank you, Shoney's, for Hot Fudge Cake. Just because.

Thank you, Bob Elbert, for singing Happy Birthday to me on the 19th day of each November. It never gets old, even if I do.

Thank you, Dex for allowing me to sit next to you when you were inducted into the Country Radio Hall of Fame. The best friends are old friends, especially old radio friends.

Larry Glass, the newspaperman who encouraged me to write. He has overcome many obstacles to operate a successful business. Plus, he's a great preacher with a large, wonderful family.

Thank you to North Jackson Progress founder Larry O. Glass, who encouraged me to write stories for him at the age of 13, and many years later, became the first to publish my weekly column. You will always be a hero to me.

Thank you to the Nigerian prince who says he's sending me a "large transfer of funds." When I disappear from public view, you'll know the check has cleared.

Thank you to whomever invented Cap'n Crunch, root beer floats, and chocolate-covered, cream-filled doughnuts. Growing older is hard enough, so we might as well have our comfort food, right?

Thank you to everyone who visits a nursing home, especially if you don't have a relative there.

Thank you, Jim Powell, radio voice of the Atlanta Braves. You're carrying on the great tradition of Ernie, Skip and Pete.

Thank you to my father-in-law, Snapper Hain. You and Anna raised a great daughter, and you're proving that 90 is the new 60.

Thank you to the Govan family of South Pittsburg, who first put me on the radio all those years ago. You sure started something.

Thank you to longtime friends and co-workers who do way too many favors for me while getting very little in return. I wish I could name you all, but I don't want to leave anyone out. You know who you are, and you know I love you.

Thank you to Stephen Geez, Ann Stewart, and the rest of Fresh Ink Group for the excellent communication, tender loving care, and patience needed to help me produce this book.

Thank you for reading my first book, and now this one. Obviously you've made it all the way to the end, so you deserve more than my thanks. You deserve a nap.

Finally:

Thank you for listening to me on the radio, watching me on TV, reading my stories, and for being my friend through the years. I once really was the kid in the candy store, and thanks to being in a career I love, I've never really left. Elton John and Bernie Taupin wrote a song that says it far better than I could express: *"I see hope in every cloud, and I'm thankful, so thankful, I've got all that I'm allowed."*

Photo Credits

Thanks to the following for graciously allowing their photos to be used:

Bob Barker 1975 publicity photo for Miss Universe Beauty Pageant photo is courtesy of CBS.

Luther Masingill portrait is courtesy of WDEF.

Ed Carter teaching photo is courtesy of North Sand Mountain High School.

Hall of Famer Greg Maddux 2009 photo by Scott R. Anselmo is courtesy of UC International.

39th president Jimmy Carter photo is courtesy of U.S. National Archives and Records Administration.

Kenny Rogers 1981 photo of performance at the University of Houston is courtesy of Special Collections, University of Houston Libraries.

"Miss Marcia" photo is courtesy of WTVC.

U.S. Rep. Marilyn Lloyd photo is courtesy of the Chattanooga Public Library, Paul Stone Collection.

Charley Pride photo courtesy of Greg Mathison, cropped from U.S. Department of Defense photo.

The Olgiati Bridge photo is courtesy of Dean Wilson.

Jim Nabors photo is courtesy of Barbara Molloy.

Dolly Parton & Porter Wagoner photo is courtesy of Moeller Talent, Inc. / Nashville (management).

Dalton Roberts photo is courtesy of the Chattanooga Public Library, Paul Stone Collection.

MaryEllen Locher photo is courtesy of John Creel.

Luther Masingill photo is courtesy of the Chattanooga Public Library, Paul Stone Collection.

Cover photo is courtesy of Mark Gilliland.

Author photo is courtesy of John Collins.

About the Author

A native of Bryant, Alabama, David Carroll has been a radio and TV personality in Chattanooga, Tennessee, for more than thirty years. He started his radio career in South Pittsburg, Tennessee, before becoming the first voice on Chattanooga's KZ-106 at the age of 21. Since then, he has reported on education issues and has anchored the evening news for almost thirty years. He is also the author of *Chattanooga Radio and Television,* which honors local broadcasting and the people who made it great. His columns are featured on ChattanoogaRadioTV.com, WRCBtv.com, and several newspapers. He is an avid fan of the Atlanta Braves and SEC football. Parents of two adult sons, Chris and Vince, David and his wife, Cindy, make their home in Chattanooga.

The Fresh Ink Group

Publishing
Free Memberships
Share & Read Free Stories, Essays, Articles
Free-Story Newsletter
Writing Contests

Books
E-books
Amazon Bookstore

Authors
Editors
Artists
Professionals
Publishing Services
Publisher Resources

Members' Websites
Members' Blogs
Social Media

www.FreshInkGroup.com

Email: info@FreshInkGroup.com

Twitter: @FreshInkGroup

Google+: Fresh Ink Group

Facebook.com/FreshInkGroup

LinkedIn: Fresh Ink Group

About.me/FreshInkGroup

CHATTANOOGA RADIO AND TELEVISION:
Images of America

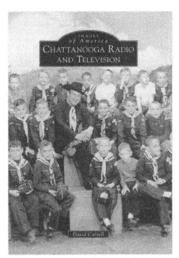

By David Carroll

To those born and raised in Chattanooga, certain names bring a smile to their faces: Miss Marcia, Bob Brandy, Mort Lloyd, Dr. Shock, and, of course, "Luther." These are among the icons of Chattanooga broadcasting. They are the faces and voices that awakened Chattanoogans each morning, delivered the news, or made them laugh. Ever since two high school pals put the city's first radio station on the air in 1925, Chattanooga has been blessed with an abundance of memorable personalities. Some passed through on their way to national fame, while others have made Chattanooga their home for more than half a century.

Growing up as a fan of these broadcasters, David Carroll was fortunate enough to become a friend and colleague to many of them as a Chattanooga radio and television personality himself. Since 1975, his career has included a stint at AM top 40 radio giant WFLI, being the first voice on FM rock station KZ-106, hosting *The Morning Show* on WDEF-TV for four years, and anchoring the evening news on WRCB-TV since 1987. He brings these people's stories to life in this wonderful collection of photos spanning then to now, providing an informative and entertaining look at Chattanooga's broadcast history.

You may order at www.ChattanoogaRadioTV.com.

ISBN 978-0-738586-85-4

BEEN THERE, NOTED THAT:

Essays In Tribute To Life

Observations, Inspiration, Remembrance, & Noteworthies To Share

By Stephen Geez

The simple lives of everyday people in a mundane world prove extraordinary in this collection of 54 personal-experience essays by novelist Stephen Geez. The eclectic mix of memoir, commentary, humor, and appreciation covers a wide range of topics, each beautifully illustrated by artists and photographers from the Fresh Ink Group. Geez catches what many of us miss, then considers how we might all share the most poignant of lessons. *Been There, Noted That* aims to reveal who we are, examine where we've been, and discover what we dare strive to become.

www.FreshInkGroup.com
ISBN: 978-1-936442-05-8

Printed in the USA
CPSIA information can be obtained
at www.ICGtesting.com
JSHW022133290224
58000JS00009B/117